HUMANA

CELEBRATING 50 YEARS OF HELPING PEOPLE

LIFELONG WELL-BEING
WELL-BEING LIFELONG

HUMANA

CELEBRATING 50 YEARS OF HELPING PEOPLE

LAURA ROWLEY

Fenwick Publishing Group, Inc.

HUMANA INC.
500 WEST MAIN STREET
LOUISVILLE, KENTUCKY 40202

WWW.HUMANA.COM

ALL IMAGES ARE FROM THE COLLECTIONS OF HUMANA INC.
AND ITS EMPLOYEES AND ALUMNI AND USED BY PERMISSION
OF HUMANA, EXCEPT FOR THOSE ON PAGES:

© BETTMANN/CORBIS: 112; KEITH BROFSKY: 27, 28-29, 47, 52-53,
62-63, 80-81, 85, 94-95, 124, 126-127, 129, 159, and 160-161; IAN
CAMPBELL PHOTOGRAPHY: 8-9, 16-17, 18, 22-23, 25, 34-35, 36,
38, 41, 44-45, 47, 48, 51, 55, 58, 72-73, 86-87, 100, 102-103, 104,
105, 106, 108-109, 110-111, 119, 120-121, 123, 128, 130, 134-135,
136, and 152-153; LIN CAUFIELD PHOTOGRAPHERS, INC.: 60-61,
67, 76, 82, 84, and 146; WENDELL CHERRY FAMILY: 14; DIANE
DAVIS: 48; JACK DEMPSEY: 144; ERICH HARTMANN MAGNUM
PHOTOS, INC.: 71 and 148; DAVID A. JONES: 12, 13, 19, 21, 25, 26,
69, 75, 92, 93, 97, 99, 156, and 157; THE KENTUCKY CENTER FOR
THE PERFORMING ARTS: 148; MILLER PUBLISHING COMPANY:
69; JOHN NATION: 150 and 151; PHOTOGRAPHY, INC.: 79;
REUTERS/BRENDAN MCDERMID: 10; THE TAMPA TRIBUNE: 31;
WAGNER INTERNATIONAL PHOTOS, INC.: 74;

ALL PHOTOGRAPHS OF ARCHIVAL PRINTS, DOCUMENTS, AND
OBJECTS WERE TAKEN BY FENWICK PUBLISHING UNLESS
OTHERWISE NOTED.

FIRST EDITION
PRINTED IN SOUTH KOREA

20 19 18 17 16 15 14 13 12 11   1 2 3 4 5

LIBRARY OF CONGRESS CATALOGING-IN-PUBLICATION DATA

ROWLEY, LAURA.
 HUMANA : CELEBRATING FIFTY YEARS OF HELPING PEOPLE / LAURA ROWLEY. -- 1ST ED.
   P. CM.
 INCLUDES INDEX.
 ISBN: 978-0-9818336-2-0
1. HUMANA, INC. 2. HEALTH INSURANCE AGENTS--UNITED STATES--HISTORY. 3. INSURANCE COMPANIES--UNITED
STATES--HISTORY. I. TITLE.
 HG9398.H8R69 2011
 368.38'2006573--DC22

2011014874

FENWICK PUBLISHING GROUP, INC.
3147 POINT WHITE DRIVE, SUITE 100
BAINBRIDGE ISLAND, WASHINGTON 98110

FENWICK PUBLISHING PRODUCES, PUBLISHES, AND MARKETS CUSTOM PUBLICATIONS FOR
CORPORATIONS, NONPROFIT ORGANIZATIONS, FAMILY FOUNDATIONS, AND INDIVIDUALS.

WWW.FENWICKPUBLISHING.COM

PRESIDENT AND PUBLISHER /// TIMOTHY J. CONNOLLY
VICE PRESIDENT /// SARAH MORGANS
DESIGN /// KEVIN BERGER WITH TARA LEE
PRODUCTION ASSISTANT /// CHARIS HENSLEY
HUMANA ARCHIVE ASSISTANT /// JORDAN REID
COPY EDITOR /// MARCO PAVIA
PROOFREADER /// BETSY HOLT
INDEXER /// KEN DELLAPENTA

FENWICK PUBLISHING EXTENDS GRATEFUL APPRECIATION TO TOM NOLAND AND ALAN PLAYER FOR
THEIR EFFORTS AND INSIGHTS DURING THE PRODUCTION OF THIS BOOK.

ABOUT THE AUTHOR:
LAURA ROWLEY IS AN AWARD-WINNING JOURNALIST SPECIALIZING IN BUSINESS AND PERSONAL
FINANCE. HER WORK HAS APPEARED ON CNN, YAHOO!FINANCE, *SELF* MAGAZINE, THE *NEW YORK
TIMES*, REALSIMPLE.COM, AND OTHER MEDIA. ROWLEY WON THE NATIONAL CLARION AWARD IN
2009 FOR BEST ONLINE COLUMN. SHE IS THE AUTHOR OF FIVE BOOKS.

FSC
www.fsc.org
MIX
Paper from
responsible sources
FSC® C005413

01

——
A COMMITMENT TO HEALTH AND WELL-BEING

FOUNDING PRINCIPLES ///

Humana founders David A. Jones (left) and H. Wendell Cherry started their first venture, a nursing home, with the belief that a focus on outcomes and efficiencies would best serve their clients. Those foundational beliefs guide Humana today.

LIFELONG WELL-BEING IS A NOBLE PURPOSE. IT ALLOWS US TO TAKE OUR CORE BUSINESS AND BROADEN THE RELATIONSHIPS WE HAVE WITH PEOPLE. WHAT ELSE CAN WE DO TO HELP PEOPLE ACHIEVE WELL-BEING?

—CHRIS TODOROFF
SENIOR VICE PRESIDENT AND GENERAL COUNSEL

FUN AND FREE ///
Carmella Belgiovine of Tamarac, Florida, pedals a cycle made available through the Freewheelin program based at her local Humana Guidance Center.

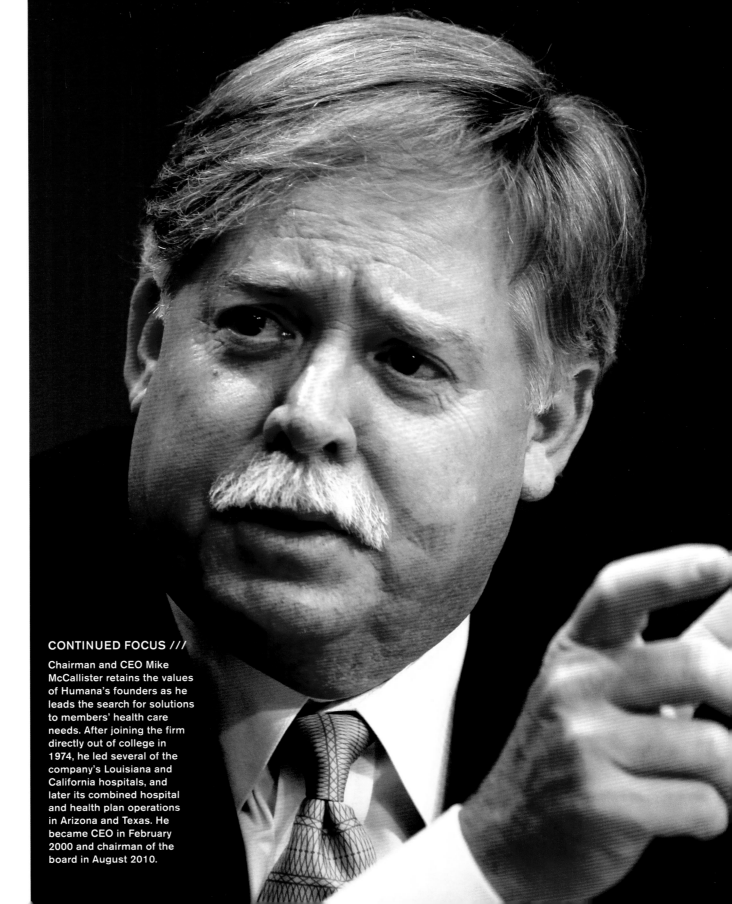

CONTINUED FOCUS ///

Chairman and CEO Mike McCallister retains the values of Humana's founders as he leads the search for solutions to members' health care needs. After joining the firm directly out of college in 1974, he led several of the company's Louisiana and California hospitals, and later its combined hospital and health plan operations in Arizona and Texas. He became CEO in February 2000 and chairman of the board in August 2010.

Founded in 1961, Humana Inc. has a diverse history—starting out as a provider of nursing home care, moving into hospitals, and ultimately entering the health insurance industry—and today offers a range of products and services for its millions of members. But a common thread runs through the story of the $34 billion, Fortune 100 company: a commitment to its members' health and well-being.

"Humana's culture is one of relentless focus on action and execution, and the company has repeatedly found a moral vision that people get behind," said Chairman and Chief Executive Officer Mike McCallister. "At the beginning, nursing homes with reliable cleanliness and quality of care were an important new addition in a time when people had new mobility in America and were living far from families. Running hospitals that were efficient and effective, and having a guarantee that a medical person would talk to you within sixty seconds of arriving at the emergency room, were big innovations we pioneered. And today in our health plans we have an emerging focus on what we can do to help people find their way in this complicated world of medicine, and improve public well-being by promoting healthy lifestyles."

Today Humana is leading the charge with a consumer-focused vision of health care, providing data-driven, personalized guidance that empowers consumers to take better care of their health and leads to lower costs. Humana is the nation's premier health benefits innovator, leveraging new products, processes, and technology that are helping to solve the fiscal crisis in American health care.

EARLY MANEUVERS ///

David A. Jones grew up in Louisville, Kentucky, and served in the U.S. Navy for three years before attending Yale Law School. He and his wife, Betty, had planned for him to attend Harvard Law School following his tour of duty, but Jones applied to Yale at the last minute in order to take a teaching position at a nearby college. Right: Jones aboard the U.S.S. *Worcester* in 1953. Below: The briefcase Jones was given upon graduation from Yale Law School. Opposite: David and Betty Jones, August 1955.

McCallister, like many of the company's thirty-five thousand associates, refers to the company's foundational values when he talks about how Louisville, Kentucky–based Humana helps its members—who are made up of seniors, members of the military, employer groups, and self-employed individuals—navigate the road ahead.

"The company was founded by entrepreneurs who were nimble, creative, and energetic," said McCallister. "From the beginning there was a constant effort to look ahead and anticipate changing strategic business needs and opportunities. The values established by our founders—integrity, accountability, and a willingness to take risks—have brought us far and will continue to be the bedrock of our success.

"Our company has focused our future around the idea of health and well-being because we know that's where the industry has to go next."

Humana was founded on the patient-focused principles of setting the highest standards of quality, efficiency, and personalized service and offering its associates the necessary tools, resources, and training to ensure their best work. Its culture is rooted in a strong commitment to integrity, innovation, continuous learning, and focused philanthropy—values first espoused fifty years ago by two ambitious Kentucky lawyers who were looking for an opportunity.

A DETOUR OF DUTY

In 1957, David A. Jones was concluding a three-year tour of duty with the U.S. Navy, and was based in New London, Connecticut. His ship, the U.S.S. *Darby*, was engaged in anti-submarine warfare tactics with the U.S.S. *Nautilus*, the world's first nuclear-powered submarine. "*Nautilus*

was quite fast and we couldn't catch it, but we were having a good time doing the best we could," said Jones.

Jones had received his bachelor's degree in 1954 from the University of Louisville, the flagship institution in his Kentucky hometown, and passed the certified public accounting exam. He and his wife, Betty, were preparing to move to Massachusetts, where he would attend Harvard Law School. But Jones, a one-time Golden Gloves boxer, had never been afraid to change course and pounce on an attractive opportunity—a trait that would come to characterize the Fortune 100 company he would eventually build with his partner, H. Wendell Cherry.

A shipmate asked Jones to accompany him to New Haven, where he had an interview at Yale Law School. While waiting for his friend, Jones noticed an ad for an accounting teacher at nearby Quinnipiac College and dashed over to apply. Jones had a child on the way, and knew Yale offered extremely affordable veterans' housing. "When I received word that I had obtained the teaching position, I applied to, and luckily was accepted by, the Yale Law School," he said.

The move was quintessential Jones: spy an opportunity, take a risk, proceed with speed and confidence, and never look back. Or to borrow a

legendary navy battle cry: damn the torpedoes, full speed ahead. Jones and future partner Cherry would spend the subsequent decades decisively seizing opportunities in a similar fashion.

Jones met Cherry in December 1959, during a job interview with Louisville law firm Wyatt, Grafton & Sloss. Cherry had just graduated from the University of Kentucky School of Law and was the newest associate. "They took me over to the Pendennis Club, which we called the 'hiring hall,' and made me an offer," Jones recalled. "I had an opportunity to visit Wendell in his office for a private discussion." In his typical forthright manner, Cherry laid out the situation. "He told me that the practice of law wasn't very much fun; that he wasn't very well paid; and he wasn't all that happy. Nonetheless I decided to join the firm."

Jones was the second of six children. His mother came from a large, well-educated though not well-off

EARLY YEARS ///

Wendell Cherry was the son of a schoolteacher and grocery wholesale business owner. While visiting Washington, D.C., with his high school basketball team, Cherry saw his first work of art, a John Singer Sargent portrait at the National Gallery. Cherry was transfixed. He would go on to support the arts and develop his own extensive collection of paintings and sculpture. Right top: Cherry, age four, at home in Horse Cave, Kentucky. Right bottom: Cherry (#21) along with his Caverna High School basketball team in the early 1950s.

chief executive of a manufacturing company) and one was an engineer. Jones's father joined the army and then worked for a manufacturing firm where his brother was an executive. In 1938, Jones's father was laid off and struggled through several years of unemployment. To ease the family's financial challenges, young David cut grass, pumped gas, clerked at a five-and-dime, and later rehabbed foreclosed homes with his brother Logan. With no money for college, Jones deferred a year and worked two jobs to save up the tuition, then joined the Navy ROTC and received a scholarship.

Wendell Cherry grew up in Horse Cave, a small town in south-central Kentucky. His mother was a schoolteacher, and his father owned a wholesale grocery company, at which Cherry worked delivering groceries to small rural stores. Bright and athletic, Cherry played high school basketball, and one year his team reached the semifinals of the state tournament. As a reward for its performance, the team took a field trip to Washington, D.C. The first stop was the National Gallery, where a painting by John Singer Sargent entranced Cherry. While the rest of the team moved on to the Smithsonian and other venues, Cherry spent the entire day in the National Gallery.

"He told me that was an epiphany for him, having never seen art of any type growing up in Horse Cave," said Jones. (Cherry later became a passionate collector, buying the famous Picasso self-portrait *Yo, Picasso*, and amassing what some critics called the nation's best collection of twentieth century sculpture, including works by Henry Moore, Alberto Giacometti, and Alexander Calder.)

Jones and Cherry became close friends almost immediately after meeting at Wyatt, Grafton & Sloss. Both were intelligent, charismatic, entrepreneurial risk-takers who shared a legendary work ethic—qualities they

Irish-American clan, and Jones's happy childhood was filled with plenty of extended family gatherings—and lots of reading. His mother, who had trained as a teacher, made weekly trips to the local library with one of her children and a wagon in tow to check out a new stack of books. At an early age, Jones discovered that education offered a powerful hedge against poverty. Two of his father's brothers were lawyers (one later became the

My relationship with Wendell was closer than that of a brother. We not only respected each other, we loved each other. We just clicked from the moment we met. It was one of those cases where opposites attract.

—DAVID A. JONES
COFOUNDER

would instill in the company they created together. Both were highly competitive and ambitious. At the same time, they were polar opposites who together formed a dynamic duo.

"They were totally different," said Rosanne Miller, who served as executive secretary to Jones for three decades. "Mr. Jones was a dreamer, and Mr. Cherry would be the one to bring the ideas down to reality; he liked to think about the details. They complemented each other very well. Mr. Jones was more social, speaking to everybody, always saying, 'Hi, I'm Dave, what's your name?' Mr. Cherry was quieter, but he could also talk up a streak, and laugh and carry on. He had a temper; it took a lot to get him riled up, but when he did, watch out. But he never held a grudge."

Jones said, "My relationship with Wendell was closer than that of a brother. We not only respected each other, we loved each other. We just clicked from the moment we met. It was one of those cases where opposites attract. We weren't cut out to be buttoned-down lawyers. Although I enjoyed legal work, Wendell hated it. He had three kids; our third child was born just before we started what became Humana. We were both poor and had growing families. We had no idea how to go about building a great company—that came as a

result of always trying to do our best at whatever we were doing."

Cherry had an artistic temperament; he was impetuous, intense, profane, and colorful, with a mischievous sense of humor. Jones was a keen observer—inventive, analytical, and diplomatic. "During our entire thirty years together, from 1961 when we started Humana until Wendell's death in July 1991, we had a wonderful and effective partnership," said Jones. "Every day, if we were both in town, we would spend an hour just talking about what was going on in the world outside Humana and how it might have an impact on our activities. Wendell was a unique thinker, with a quick and decisive mind that he focused on the steady flow of ideas that I produced. He could, and did, spot losers quickly, and his judgment helped us avoid unpromising initiatives."

Shortly after Jones joined the Wyatt firm, the two Kentucky lawyers began dabbling in new construction projects, including building a small, successful subdivision in suburban Okolona, and an unsuccessful Holiday Inn just south of Elizabethtown. But it would be a nursing home venture that would establish their foundation in the health care industry and solidify their lifelong partnership.

LISTENING TO UNDERSTAND ///

Humana's top priority is making health care understandable to its members so that they are in the best position to make good choices for lifelong well-being. This guidance often comes over the telephone, so call operations is a critical mission. Natalie Gaunce (facing), director of customer care operations, meets with Dee Radford, the process manager for Medicare call operations, at the company's Louisville headquarters to discuss ways to improve processes and performance at Medicare call centers around the country.

The two men assembled a team of investors, and at a time when professional facilities were the exception rather than the rule, developed Heritage House, a seventy-eight-bed nursing home on a two-acre site in Louisville. It opened in August 1962 and quickly set a standard for smart design and personalized service.

For several months, Jones and Cherry managed the nursing home while working long hours at the Wyatt law firm and teaching night courses at the University of Louisville. David A. Jones, Jr., was a preschooler at the time. "We had a little tiny room—really a closet—off of our kitchen, where my dad had set up a desk," Jones Jr. recalled from his childhood. "He kept the books until the company got large enough to hire an accountant. He had an old hand-cranked calculator with paper tape, and every evening after dinner you'd hear the clickety-clack of him entering the figures and keeping the spreadsheets."

Jones contrasted his low-key management style with Cherry's. "In the early days, Wendell and I were running the place, and I would hire the nurses in the morning and Wendell would fire them in the evening, reflecting a difference in our personalities," Jones joked. "Before long we had enough patients in the facility to break even." (It was so successful, in fact, that additions were constructed a year later and also in 1967.)

In 1964, Jones and Cherry constructed a second successful facility in nearby Lexington and quickly assembled investor partnerships to build new nursing homes in New Haven and Waterbury, Connecticut, and Virginia Beach, Virginia. The same year, they negotiated a buyout of some of the partners and incorporated as Heritage House of America. By 1967, the company owned eight nursing homes and went public, providing a significant cash infusion to expand nationwide. Jones left the Wyatt firm to start his own

A RAPID START ///

When Cherry, left bottom, and Jones, left top, started out in the nursing home industry, they handled many issues themselves while maintaining their jobs at the law firm where they first met. Jones would keep the nursing home books in an alcove off his family's kitchen. As the nursing home business took off and their company went public, they left the Wyatt law firm and began buying up nursing homes all around the country. Today, Humana operates out of an award-winning high-rise in downtown Louisville. Opposite: A cross-functional group of clinical and digital team members meeting about the clinical user experience of the Humana Vitality program in the Louisville headquarters.

practice, which he managed along with the nursing home. Cherry quickly followed.

INSPIRING A TEAM

Soon Jones, Cherry, and Carl Pollard, who had joined the firm as head of finance, were buying nursing homes all over the country. "I went home and told my dad I was changing jobs, and these were the two smartest guys I'd ever met," said Pollard, who was eventually promoted to senior executive vice president. "They were bright, ambitious, full of energy, and weren't afraid to take a risk. In 1968, the stock came out at eight dollars and went to eighty dollars, and we were smart enough to know that wasn't going to last forever, so we used that currency to buy hard assets. They gave me tremendous latitude, and I promise you I had no idea what I was doing."

Rosanne Miller shared a similar experience. "If you did well with an assignment you would get a bigger project the next time," she recalled. "The company allowed you to grow and learn. I learned that if a problem or situation arises, it's very helpful to have a few possible solutions before you tell the boss. They always wanted you to be thinking. The more skills you developed, the more responsibility you were given. It was really an environment of lifetime learning."

That trust and empowerment inspired loyalty in the staff that joined the nascent firm. Joan Hester, a thirty-two-year Humana veteran, started as Jones's secretary at the Wyatt firm directly out of high school in July 1960. She later served as Cherry's assistant for more than two decades. "People had a sense of partnership because that's how we were treated—as equals," Hester said. Hester said Jones would patiently explain a task—such as locating real estate documents at the courthouse—and then delegate the job to her. "We all just pitched in and did what needed to be done. Mr. Jones and Mr. Cherry had a way of winning people over. These men were such exciting people; they had a real charisma about them. They never failed to let us know they appreciated our work and gave us lots of credit. We knew they really cared about us, and that motivated us."

Charlie Teeple, who served Humana for twenty-three years as vice president of investor relations and communications, agreed. "I think they inspired people like a football coach does—after they finished talking, you were ready to go out and run through a brick wall." Jones, in fact, had coached both a football team and a basketball

team in the navy. "I learned that not all people have the same motivation or ambition," Jones explained. "It was a surprise to me, because I had thought everyone was as competitive as I was. But I learned a lot about how you make a team out of people who bring different skills."

The company also provided family-friendly work policies that were decades ahead of their time. Wanda Ryan joined the firm in 1966 at age nineteen as an executive assistant. "After I got married and had my first child, Mr. Jones told me I could work four days a week,"

Ryan said. "When I had my second child, I was going to quit, and he talked me into staying one day a week. Then I came back two, three, and four days, and then full-time. He made it easy to continue working for him. Mr. Jones as a rule has always been very loyal to people." Ryan worked for Jones for forty-five years before retiring in 2011.

Part of that policy may have been inspired by Jones's childhood: his mother had a teaching degree, but was precluded from teaching by laws that made it illegal for married women in Kentucky to teach in public school. "In the early days we were very democratic," Jones admitted. "If we lost an executive secretary, we wouldn't hire a new one—we would promote the best secretary in the organization. The person who lost their staff member didn't like it, but the secretaries liked it and went on to great jobs in the company."

Cherry wrote the company philosophy in brief—"People Before Paper"—and had it framed and mounted on his office wall. "Those of us who were associated with Wendell Cherry for a number of years, and at least think we knew him well, will never forget the most endearing aspects of his personality—his quick wit, warm sense of humor, and genuine charm," Hester wrote in a book of essays honoring Cherry after his death. "He possessed an incredible ability to laugh at himself and always enjoyed a good joke." In the same book, Pollard recalled an instance of Cherry's humor at a meeting with investment bankers. It took place at an airport hotel restaurant known for its strolling violinists. "When the violinists arrived near our table, Wendell gave them fifty dollars to go away and another fifty dollars to stop playing altogether," Pollard wrote.

William Ballard, Jr., Humana's executive vice president and chief financial officer from 1970 to 1992, met Cherry in the late 1960s for an interview before he joined the law firm Jones had founded. "The meeting took place at lunch, and I remember that I was treated to a one-hour monologue from Wendell on University of Kentucky basketball," he recalled in the book of essays. "Wendell continued this interviewing technique over the next twenty-two years. He regaled job candidates, who generally left the encounter with a desire to join Humana and an appreciation for Wendell's infectious enthusiasm."

Ryan added, "They always cared about the people that were working for them; they were very considerate and very fair." Jones could not afford to give her a raise when she followed him from the Wyatt law firm to Heritage House, so they compensated her with two hundred shares of stock. "If I had held onto them I could have retired much sooner, but unfortunately I did not," Ryan said.

Miller said the company was like family. "I grew up there, and it was a very stabilizing force for me. Two years after I started I got a call from somewhere I had applied and was offered a 50 percent raise. I cried all the way to the interview. I was so relieved they didn't offer me the job, and I never went to another interview again." Her loyalty paid off: "I went to work for Mr. Jones in 1981, and I was in the place I had dreamed of, working in the CEO's office."

A CAN-DO PHILOSOPHY

Jones and Cherry hired Linden McLellan to serve as assistant vice president at the Heritage House firm. McLellan had come from a six-year stint with the Internal Revenue Service and was hired as controller and director of feasibility studies for new locations.

**FOCUSED
ATTENTION ///**

When members call
Humana with questions,
they are routed to the
appropriate specialists
to focus on their
needs. Louisville-based
customer service
representatives Ronnita
Nebbitt (foreground) and
Yolanda McElroy provide
support to Medicare
members seeking
information on their
enrollment applications
or billing statements.

I remember David Jones looking me dead in the eye, and he said, "Bill, business is tough—tough as it can be, but when it's tough, you look forward. Never do anything that causes you to have to look back over your shoulder to see if someone is coming after you."

—BILL BALLARD
FORMER CHIEF FINANCIAL OFFICER

"I joined the company on April 3, 1967, and quickly discovered you had to be flexible," McLellan recalled. "Within the first hour of reporting to work I was to take a package to New York and have it at a certain office by 3:00 p.m. that day. I did, and made it on time. I quickly discovered that 'cannot do' was not an acceptable response to the founders of this company. They had a strong 'can do' philosophy, which never changed during my career with the company. I suspect that philosophy still prevails to this day."

Bill Baldwin, director of information technology acquisitions for Humana, started in 1970. He confirmed that the philosophy does indeed prevail more than forty years later: "They were a tough group, never-say-die. They had a lot of conviction. That's what drove the company: they got a vision, marched toward it, and succeeded. The mantra from the top was 'don't be afraid to go off and conquer new things.' It's the same today with [Chairman and CEO] Mike McCallister. He's got a vision, and we're all marching toward that."

Along with a can-do attitude, Jones and Cherry insisted associates treat nursing home patients like family members. "They both strove for perfection, and they didn't shortcut on anything. Patient care was paramount on the list, and they were very proud of that," Baldwin recalled. "We all thought of our work as a noble business."

The firm's 1969 annual report noted: "Excellent care for the patient remains our primary consideration. Cost reduction doesn't mean lowering the standards of patient care. It means such things as cutting purchasing costs through negotiation of national contracts with suppliers, holding down the number of clerical associates through the use of a computer in our centralized accounting system, and operating food service, laundry, and housekeeping departments in an efficient and business-like manner."

Former chief financial officer Ballard remembered meeting, in his first months with the company, with Jones about an accounting issue. "I don't know what the issue was, but I remember David Jones looking me dead in the eye, and he said, 'Bill, business is tough—tough as it can be, but when it's tough, you look forward. Never do anything that causes you to have to look back over your shoulder to see if someone is coming after you.' And Humana never did. We were the most honest, straightforward company there was. We always looked forward, and David made it clear that everything you did was to be ethical. That was always our guiding principle."

Integrity has always been a fundamental company value, noted Jones. "I think that everything depends

In 1968, the company, whose name was changed to Extendicare, agreed to lease a hospital under construction in Huntsville, Alabama. A year later, the firm purchased five hospitals, including a new facility under construction. The partners moved with characteristic confidence, seeking to acquire other top-notch hospitals. David A. Jones, Jr., looked at a facility with his father and Wendell Cherry. "We were down in Florida on vacation in the early 1970s, and they were looking at a hospital," Jones Jr recalled. "I was thirteen or fourteen years old. My dad said, 'Hey, do you want to come?' So we met up with Mr. Cherry and I just tagged along, and someone presumably in administration met us and started showing us around. We couldn't have been more than twenty feet inside the entrance when Mr. Cherry stopped, put his hands on a door frame, and said, 'David, this is a dump; we don't want this hospital,' and he turned around and walked out. They were really decisive."

Some industry observers criticized the expansions of for-profit operators, but Jones said their objections never made sense to him. "You can't achieve the moral high ground by assertion—you can only achieve it by performance," he said. "We achieved wonderful humanitarian success, but it was through performance. There is nothing about failure to pay taxes that lends moral weight to a hospital. If hospitals aren't run for performance, they are wasting societal resources." In 1983, for example, after Medicare changed its reimbursement system, Humana's hospitals were so efficiently run that they cost the federal program 25 percent less than their nonprofit peers. "Medicare was paying us 75 percent of what they paid nonprofits. Our cost structure gave us a profit margin and that's what enabled us to

on leadership—that's what builds a great enterprise." Jones continued, "If the leader cheats, that says it's okay for everyone in the organization to do it. You can't put integrity in someone—it comes from the way they were brought up, and a person who lacks integrity will get into trouble at some point." With guiding principles of honesty, innovation, and a spirit of renewal, Cherry and Jones began moving away from nursing homes and into a new venture in the late 1960s: hospitals.

Hospital demand was enormous. Research indicated that $20 billion to $30 billion of hospital construction was needed in the early 1970s to serve an expanding population and replace aging and outdated facilities.

The fragmented, localized hospital industry also cried out for management efficiency. Across the Southeast, area physicians constructed small town hospitals. "The doctors built the hospitals because they needed a place to put patients, not because they wanted to run hospitals," Ballard explained. "With Medicare, they saw their lives getting more complex, and they wanted out so they could just practice medicine. We provided liquidity and took the responsibility of running the hospitals."

extendicare
skilled nursing centers

grow. Profit is never an end in itself; it's the cost of being prepared for the unknowns of the future," said Jones.

The Humana commitment to excellence engendered strong cost discipline. The national average cost of hospital construction in 1974 was $67,000 per bed, according to Blue Cross and Blue Shield Plans. That year Humana completed fourteen hospitals. The average cost of the Humana hospitals—including land, buildings, equipment, interest during construction, and all the other expenditures necessary for a first-quality hospital—was $34,089 per bed, or just about half the national average. "The major difference is largely explained by the fact that most newly constructed hospitals are designed and supervised by administrators and trustees who have never before been responsible for such a project, a fact that tends to raise costs without raising quality," the 1975 annual report stated. "In contrast, Humana's new hospital project costs benefit from its growing expertise in design and construction supervision, gained in the completion, to date, of thirty-three hospitals."

A CONSUMER-FOCUSED APPROACH

Equally important, Humana took a consumer-focused approach to hospital care—a strategy that would later provide the foundation and direction for its insurance business. Executives began measuring every aspect of hospital operations to establish benchmarks for quality and continually monitor them for control and management. "We wanted to be the best and spent a lot of time and money to measure care," said Pollard. "All the hospitals said they gave good patient care, but we asked, 'What's the standard?' And there was none for all practical purposes."

Humana began to evaluate all aspects of hospital operations, using time and motion studies to capture hours of patient care per floor and per wing. The company studied rates of infection; the number of retakes on X-rays; how many times a phlebotomist had to prick a patient to draw blood; and whether all its surgeons were using double gloves, Pollard recalled. In addition, the company listened to its customers—sending patients surveys following their release from the hospital, which were collected at headquarters rather than at each location to ensure proper follow-up. "I would say 80 to 90 percent of the time if you saw a pattern on questionnaires that came back, after an investigation, by and large the customers were right," said Pollard. "That prompted us to start applying a more sophisticated standard."

The hospitals had to conform to "the five Cs," recalled Charlie Teeple, former vice president for investor relations and communications. "Our professionals had to be cheerful, compassionate, courteous, and competent, and all the hospitals had to be clean. Humana is a company that is customer-driven. It was built on meeting customer needs. To be a part of this wonderful corporation as it grew was very satisfying. I had a great uncle who worked for Thomas Edison and another great uncle who was head auditor at General Electric. They were part of the beginnings of marvelous enterprises, and I had the same feeling when I was working at Humana."

By the end of fiscal 1975, Humana owned sixty hospitals with 7,800 beds in fifteen states and was the second-largest investor-owned hospital service company in the U.S. The firm employed nearly fourteen thousand people. The 1975 annual report proclaimed a new mission statement: "To achieve and maintain, through a system of hospital management, an unequaled level of measurable quality and productivity, in the delivery of hospital services which are responsive to the values and needs of patients and their physicians."

AN INCLUSIVE CULTURE

Humana's culture was characterized by hard work and camaraderie, acknowledged Charlene Coultas, who was hired in 1971 as a nursing home bookkeeper and is now a data analyst. "Everything was calculators and spreadsheets. We worked long hours to balance the books and file government reports at the end of the year," she recalled, adding that Jones and Cherry ran a tight ship. "Our calculators had paper tapes, and they would rewind the paper and use the other side the next day. Everybody worked on one floor, and [Jones and Cherry] would walk through the office and say, 'What are you working on?' And you'd best be there working hard. But they were very generous. They would give us bonuses, remember birthdays, and host an annual Christmas party. It was fun—you felt like you were part of the team." In the early days, most of the staff would head over to the YMCA at lunchtime, the men to play basketball and the women to run on the track or play racquetball, Coultas recalled. Office teams competed in softball, track, and golf leagues, and played volleyball at the company picnic.

**GUIDANCE FOR
LARGE GROUPS ///**

Some of Humana's
health care products
are provided as group
plans through employers.
Through these, Humana
helps employers
control costs, provide
a range of choices to
their employees, and
administer benefits.
Damon Young (facing)
director of account
management for large
employers, provides
background to new
associate Andrew
Reinbold, who joined
the Chicago office as
a regional marketing
consultant.

Rosanne Miller joined the company in May 1974. "When the company was small we were together a lot," noted Miller. "In the 1970s, we had an annual dinner dance in November, and everyone in the company was invited. You could bring your spouse or guest, and the chairman's awards were handed out. Mr. Jones selected the winners from nominations made by supervisors. That was always a huge deal. Even back then I think the award was $1,000, and the winners got their pictures in the company newsletter."

As the company grew, Jones and Cherry turned to management guru Peter Drucker to shape their human resources strategy. In 1974, Cherry had been stuck in a New York airport and had picked up a book by Drucker. Jones recalled, "He called me and said, 'Some guy named Drucker has written a book about us.' It was filled with wisdom and covered the kinds of issues we were dealing with. We went to California and spent two days with him, and went every year for many years after that. One of the things he taught us was that a successful enterprise must create conditions that allow associates to do their best work. To do that you provide tools people need, including education. That became a basic tenet of the Humana philosophy. It's also the greatest marketing tool there is: if doctors believe that Hospital A will give them a better platform to do their best work than Hospital B, then they will send their patients to Hospital A." Jones later became the founding chair of the Drucker School of Management at Claremont College.

Humana recruited associates from the colleges near its hospitals and internally promoted candidates to be hospital administrators and financial managers, training them in a program divided between classroom sessions in the corporate headquarters and on-the-job experience in various positions in hospitals. As a result, program graduates were thoroughly trained in Humana's people-oriented standards by the time they advanced to management positions. "Every year we hired a whole bunch of bright young people," explained Jones. "Sometimes they had degrees in hospital management, but we would also take someone with a degree in music or philosophy if they were bright and energetic. We would hire the top graduates of colleges in areas where we were operating, putting them to work in neighborhoods where they were culturally acclimated already, and then transfer them later on as their skills grew. By hiring from Louisiana Technical University we ran into Mike McCallister," who became an analyst in the finance department in 1974. He was named CEO in February 2000 and chairman of the board in August 2010.

As Humana grew, Jones said, "We tried to keep the organization as flat as possible so ideas had a chance to be heard." Jones implemented a weekly management committee meeting of the top five or six officers of the company. "We promised people out in the field that if they had a request that required capital for something they wanted to do, they could complete the staff work and make their case, and we would give a decision that week. And we kept that promise." If Jones or Cherry were out of town, another executive would step in to make the decision. "We didn't believe in the notion that one person is so omnipotent that only that person can make the decisions. Most decisions can be made by any capable or informed person. One of the great things about Humana—and it continues today under the leadership of Mike McCallister—is that decisions are not delayed. That's a terrible defect of most bureaucracies. I learned in law school that justice delayed is justice denied, and the same is true of ideas. People were empowered to offer to change anything going on in the company. If you didn't like our way you could come up with another way, and it would get a hearing."

Regina Nethery, vice president of investor relations, said that tradition of openness continues today with McCallister: "There's an 'Ask Mike' e-mail box that allows associates to share their thoughts. The general culture in meetings is that no one is thought to be unworthy of making a comment in a meeting; if there are twenty people in the room and you have a thought, you speak your thought. You don't have to think, 'Well, I'm not an executive.' It's a respectful and collaborative environment."

In addition, Humana established a unique grievance procedure. Associates who had an issue could appeal through several levels of management and ultimately take the matter before Jones if it wasn't resolved. "If there was unfairness, it could, with persistence, come to my attention," said Jones. "It had an amazing impact. With tens of thousands of associates we never had a union movement because we treated people fairly, and every single person who wasn't treated fairly could have their issue heard. Not many came to me, because the executives didn't want me to think they couldn't solve a problem. But it gave people the assurance that Humana

was a fair employer. The few cases that got to me were so balanced they could have fallen either way."

Susan Kaus, an account advisor, joined the firm in 1973 as a nurse's aide. "The feedback, the benefits, the managers, the ethics training that we get—all of that helps you to see that this is a company that really cares about you," she said. "I've had wonderful managers through all my years. Even when jobs were being eliminated, you were not out in the cold because they would help you to find something else. So it's a little bit of everything that shows me they care."

Leigh Speiden, who works in Humana's national education department and joined the firm in the early 1970s, agreed. "They have been very good to me and I've been very lucky," she said. "People show appreciation for the work I've done, and for me that's the biggest difference: that you've added value, and you're improving something. People here are committed to doing a good job. They are invested in what they do and what they produce, and that makes it an exciting, dynamic organization."

Through rapid growth and strategic acquisitions, Humana became the world's largest investor-owned hospital company. In 1980, a dozen years after Humana had leased its first facility in Alabama, the company owned ninety hospitals in twenty-three states and two European countries, and reported revenues in excess of $1 billion—the first company in its industry to surpass that milestone. It would maintain its principles of productivity, quality, collaboration, and most important, a consumer-oriented focus as it began to make its next strategic shift: into health insurance.

OPEN-DOOR POLICY ///

Throughout Humana's fifty years in operation, its leaders have sought ways in which associates at all levels of the company can be heard. Under founders David A. Jones and Wendell Cherry, associates were empowered to make executive-level decisions in their absence. Later, Jones established a grievance procedure that allowed associates' concerns to reach his desk if not resolved satisfactorily. That tradition continues under the leadership of Mike McCallister, left, who instituted an "Ask Mike" e-mail box where associates can send their thoughts and questions.

02

—

EMPOWERING CONSUMERS

CALLING THE SHOTS ///

The members of Humana's Management Committee—shown here in the early 1980s—met every Tuesday morning at 9:30. Present at this meeting were (clockwise from left) Carl Pollard, executive vice president; Wendell Cherry; David A. Jones; Thomas Flynn, executive vice president and general counsel; Bill Ballard, executive vice president, finance and administration; and Henry Werronen, senior vice president, marketing.

OUR JOB IS TO FIGURE OUT HOW TO HELP PHYSICIANS AND CONSUMERS MAKE BETTER DECISIONS SO THEY USE THE THINGS THEY GET THE MOST VALUE OUT OF AND STAY AWAY FROM THE THINGS THAT DON'T ADD VALUE.

—TOM LISTON
SENIOR VICE PRESIDENT, SENIOR PRODUCTS

CARING INSTRUCTION
Newly hired associate Grant Horton receives training to become a
personal health coordinator for Humana Cares. The St. Petersburg–based
health support service is provided primarily to chronically ill members of
Humana's health plans for seniors.

PERSONAL SERVICE ///

Humana members can
receive in-person attention to
their questions and concerns
at Humana's Guidance
Centers throughout the
country. Lora and Joe Cole
discuss questions about
their coverage with sales
agent Randy Garrett at the
Humana Guidance Center in
Zephyrhills, Florida.

In 2002, thirty-three-year-old Cheryl Brock found herself shopping online for insurance benefits after her employer introduced new health plan options, including a "consumer-driven health plan" (CDHP). That's a high-deductible plan linked to a tax-advantaged health savings account (HSA). Brock chose a Humana plan that covered her first $500 worth of health care spending; after that she was responsible for costs up to $2,000. Then traditional insurance would kick in to pay 100 percent of the balance of her medical costs. Brock could save up money to cover her deductible in the HSA—and receive matching funds from her employer up to a certain amount. Money that wasn't spent could be rolled toward the next year's health care costs. Moreover, preventive care—such as checkups—would be free under the plan.

Brock's monthly insurance premium fell by 75 percent to $10, saving her $360 a year. Brock was willing to take the risk that she could keep her health care spending below $500. "Depending on what the doctor wanted to test me for and why, I would determine whether I want to do that," she told a *USA Today* reporter. "It's my responsibility to evaluate the cost of health care."

In 2005, when Kansas retiree Dave Major was on the verge of turning sixty-five, he researched a range of Medicare health maintenance organizations (HMOs) through his county's Department of Aging. In the 1980s, in an effort to make Medicare more cost-efficient, Congress had implemented a program allowing retirees to enroll in private HMOs, which are

paid a predetermined amount by the government to provide all Medicare-covered services to enrollees. Major chose the Humana Gold Choice Plan, which included free exercise classes at his local YMCA through its "SilverSneakers" program.

"The SilverSneakers program has been my favorite part of Gold Choice," Major wrote to Humana. "I have attended three times a week since November 2005. We stretch, lift weights, and use a resistance band, all to lively music. When holidays come around we stay for lunch and some socializing. Humana furnishes the main dishes and the door prize. My cholesterol count has come down thirty-nine points, and I feel better than I have in years. Two years ago I could work on my antique cars in the yard for a half day at the most. Now I go all day long and am ready for more the next day."

Dave Major and Cheryl Brock are emblematic of Humana's pioneering strategy to put consumers at the center of health care decision-making, and to facilitate choices that improve their well-being as well as save them money. Humana's consumer-focused strategy, launched at the turn of the twenty-first century, lies at

the core of both its philosophy and its products for seniors, employer groups, self-employed individuals, and members of the military.

Humana Chairman and CEO Mike McCallister believed that individual consumers could be agents of change for a broken health care system. In fact, the word *system* is a misnomer, McCallister argued. "A system has certain attributes. There are usually connected incentives intended to align a lot of processes, and ongoing process improvement. Many times technology is involved, there is a lot of data, and most of the time the system is transparent in what it does and how it functions," he explained. "Health care has none of that—it's not connected, there's little data transparency around quality and productivity, and incentives are not aligned. We have the best health care in the world in the United States, if you can get to it and pay for it. But we certainly don't have a system, because it is in no way connected."

The dysfunction in the current model can be traced to a historical accident: the rise of employer-based insurance benefits. "The model comes from the post–World War II period when the federal government

> **The model comes from the post—World War II period when the federal government enacted wage controls. Companies gave employees health benefits because they couldn't give them more cash.**
>
> **—JIM BLOEM**
> CHIEF FINANCIAL OFFICER AND TREASURER

enacted wage controls," said Jim Bloem, Humana's chief financial officer and treasurer. "Companies gave employees health benefits because they couldn't give them more cash." The system was institutionalized in the 1950s after Congress provided employers with a tax break for these benefits. "It's one of the few places in the U.S. tax code where the employer gets a deduction but the employee doesn't pick up income," Bloem added.

Twenty years after the war, the government modeled Medicare and Medicaid on this comprehensive-insurance model, and a year later had enrolled nearly 12 percent of the population. Thus, a system developed in which very few consumers of health services were primarily responsible for paying for them.

With economic incentives wildly askew, health care costs exploded in the subsequent decades, devouring 18 percent of U.S. gross domestic product by 2010, up from 7 percent in 1970. Medicare and Medicaid spending swelled from 1 percent of the federal budget in 1966 to 20 percent in 2010, and continues to escalate. "If you look at how people who provide health care earn money, the more they do the more they are paid—so that's an incentive to do more work," McCallister explained. "Studies indicate that up to 50 percent of all health care delivered in this country is of no added value.

Many people are over-treated—they get the wrong thing at the wrong time for the wrong reason. Then look at the buying of health care: most people don't pay for their own health care services. To the extent that employers are trying to finance all of the health care that employees and their providers can dream up and think they need, you don't have any of the normal economic incentives in place that drive the productivity and efficiency we see in the rest of the economy. Many people don't have the motivation to seek out the best value as they would in the rest of their consumer lives, and there is no transparency around price and quality. Over time, in every other industry, you always get lower prices and higher quality because of better information, technology, and constant improvement. In the rest of the economy this is very powerful—bad products and services are crushed by consumers. In health care not only do they not get crushed—they get paid for every day."

Consider the way consumer empowerment has disrupted other industries: car buyers can research and compare the features and costs of vehicles online before stepping foot in a dealership, fully prepared to negotiate the best deal. Stockbrokers have been replaced by online trading sites, accountants by TurboTax software, and travel agents by a plethora of booking web sites. All of these developments have reduced costs and improved speed and service, requiring traditional providers to follow suit. Although purchasing health care is clearly more complex than buying a car or booking a trip to Europe, patients armed with better information can make smarter decisions. A knee-surgery patient who can go online to find out how many procedures local hospitals have done, how often they resulted in complications, and what they cost is better prepared to act in his self-interest. A patient who is notified that a cheaper but similarly effective generic alternative drug exists can discuss it with her doctor and save money.

Thus, McCallister decided the only way to achieve a long-term cost solution was by unleashing the power of the patients, who were becoming increasingly motivated to act. "As cost-sharing is becoming greater with higher deductibles, people now have more of a financial stake in their health care decisions," said McCallister. "It feels like a bad thing, but in terms of the larger policy implication, it's a good thing. When people start spending more of their own money, they will begin to ask, 'What is that for? Do I really need it? What is the cost? Do I have a choice of location where I can get it, and what are implications of price and quality?'"

Consumer empowerment is the foundation of the company's Medicare Advantage business, which today accounts for most of its profitability and growth. "What I like about the Medicare business is that you have to take whoever signs up and then figure out a way to take care of them, to keep them healthy, which helps to keep cost down," said Tom Liston, senior vice president, senior

products, who started as an outside auditor for Humana in 1983 and joined the firm in 1995. "It is a consumer-friendly business focused on delivering innovative services. We have hundreds of nurses and physicians who are talking to people on the phone every day, helping them navigate the delivery system to get better outcomes. The more we can help people do the right things with their physician to get the best preventive care, the better value they can get out of the system."

Liston recounted a discussion with a Harvard medical school professor who estimated that 25 to 50 percent of the procedures performed in the delivery of health care do not affect patient outcomes. "We spend $2.6 trillion on health care in the U.S. Let's say one third of services—or more than $850 billion—is not contributing to the outcome, but is wasted money that could be spent for other things. It only costs $700 billion a year to feed the nation. We are likely wasting more in health care than it costs to feed the nation. Our job is to figure out how to help physicians and consumers make better decisions so they use the things they get the most value out of and stay away from the things that don't add value. There is good evidence-based medicine that has proven certain things work. But the variation in practice patterns around the country is so broad that by definition everyone can't be performing the best practice."

Humana has developed a goal for its Medicare Advantage business called the "15 Percent Solution." By targeting waste and inefficiency, providing services to encourage members to stay healthy, and offering coordinating care for the frailest seniors, the company believes it can deliver better care at 15 percent below the cost of the public program managed by the government. "We have decided our profit margin over the long term will stay at 5 percent, and the extra 10 percent will be reinvested in strategies and services that motivate

members or physicians to focus on preventive care," said Liston. "We will reward them for that or invest the savings back into the product design, which will make deductibles and co-pays lower for members."

In the next seven years, ten million more people will be eligible for Medicare, so Humana expects continued growth with the aging population, even if funding for the program shrinks. "But it's all dependent on getting the best value out of the delivery system," said Liston. "There's so much fat in there that we believe we can provide better benefits and do it at a cost that's at or below Medicare by doing it in the right way and not the old HMO heavy-handed way. We help consumers make better decisions by providing real-time, personalized, and relevant information."

Inspiring consumers to take charge of their own health is core to Humana's larger vision of promoting the full spectrum of well-being, which the company defines as living happily with a balanced sense of purpose, belonging, security, and health. "Lifelong well-being is a noble purpose," said Chris Todoroff, senior vice president and general counsel. "It allows us to take our core business and broaden the relationships we have with people. What else can we do to help people achieve well-being? That will drive the expansion of the kinds of products and services we offer going forward."

THE BEGINNINGS OF CONSUMER-FOCUSED HEALTH INSURANCE

In 1983, Humana launched a health maintenance organization (HMO) designed to help employers and unions control their premium costs by guaranteeing a cap on increases for several years while giving participants the same benefits and freedom to choose their doctors. If hospital or outpatient services were required, the members would have significant incentives to choose Humana hospitals. The business mushroomed from both organic growth and acquisitions, and by the end of the 1980s health plans had become a billion-dollar business with more than a million members. Humana employed more than 55,000 people.

But ultimately, a conflict arose between its hospitals and insurance plans, and in 1993 Humana spun off the hospitals into a new entity, Galen Health Care.

TAKING ADVANTAGE OF TECHNOLOGY ///

Around the same time that Mike McCallister transitioned into the role of CEO, Humana's leadership was exploring ways to take advantage of technologies like next-generation paperless health plans. Right: Mike McCallister (right) speaks with David A. Jones in 2001, the year after McCallister was named chief executive.

Humana became solely a health insurance company and found itself struggling in a business in which competitors slashed prices, took on losses to gain market share, and then raised premiums—practices that did nothing to address the fundamental problem: skyrocketing health care costs. At a 1999 board meeting, Humana's leaders presented a vision of next-generation paperless health plans to the Board of Directors. The internet-based plans were intended to transform Humana into a high-tech, high-touch infomediary for its members—the earliest vision of a new kind of health services company.

Simultaneous with the development of its new digital health plan, Humana was wrestling with its own burgeoning health care costs, which were rising faster than the national average. In 2000, when McCallister was named chief executive, costs for the firm's 14,500 associates were projected to rise 19 percent year-over-year and were forecast for double-digit increases in the future. "We were trying to answer a very, very big question: 'What would it take to rationalize the cost of health care in the U.S.?'" McCallister explained in a 2006 podcast interview with the Wharton School of Business at the University of Pennsylvania. "We started putting down everything that's been tried, everything that's failed, everything that's worked—there haven't been too many things that have worked. When we started listing the history of it, all the various approaches that people have tried to apply over many, many years, it quickly became clear that the one thing no one had ever tried was to get the consumer at the heart of this."

One of the problems in health care had been a "one size fits all" approach, McCallister told Wharton interviewers: "I would stipulate that the consumer is very complex, that people need and want different things . . . and it's interesting that the rest of the economy responds to that every single day. Consumers drive everything— except in health care, where people try to do a top-down approach to these folks. If you don't get down to their individual level and meet their needs, find out what they are going to respond to, the chance that collectively they're going to change anything is zero."

McCallister envisioned an approach to health care governed by five principles: consumerism, wellness, financial literacy, health stewardship, and shared responsibility. First, a health plan should motivate members to determine the value, quality, and effectiveness of care before they buy it, and be rewarded financially for doing so. Second, wellness programs had to be a core component of the strategy, because analyses had found about 20 percent of plan participants accounted for the majority of costs, including people with chronic conditions such as diabetes, obesity, and tobacco addiction. Thus, the plan had to offer incentives to encourage participants to favor healthy lifestyles, control their weight, quit smoking, and boost physical activity. Third, financial literacy required that participants receive the tools and information to accurately analyze the cost of their options—and invest the time to do so. (Studies showed the average worker spent just sixteen minutes each year choosing benefits.) Fourth, Humana would facilitate health stewardship by providing information about health and disease management, as well as data about the quality and success rates of

hospitals, doctors, and other providers. Finally, shared responsibility meant the employer should make clear to associates that they would have protection from major health care expenses, but must bear their share of the cost. Health insurance would shift toward the models of auto or homeowner plans: the employee would cover the health care equivalents of door dings or broken windows, and the employer, a collision or fire.

Moreover, Humana's relationship with customers would change. Under the old HMO model, health insurers served as gatekeepers, telling members what health care professionals they could see, what treatments they could get, and what drugs they could take. The system was confusing and frustrating, and inspired little loyalty among members and health care professionals. In addition, the data didn't support the notion that restrictive policies worked.

Humana approved some 98.5 percent of all preauthorization requests, for example, thus paying huge costs— both administratively and in terms of goodwill—to achieve relatively small savings. The new consumer-centric care model would replace those restrictions with options.

McCallister also recognized the power of the web in managing and delivering the complexity of those options. "Even in 2000, it was clear that people were going to do significant transactional work over the Internet; that people were going to seek out information on the Internet; and they were going to use the Internet for comparisons and for better pricing on products," McCallister told the Wharton interviewers.

PREPARING TO LEAD ///

The clinical and non-clinical staff who provide health guidance and education to members undergo rigorous training and ongoing enrichment throughout their careers. Charis Gallaty, quality assurance clinical process specialist, updates materials before a training session for personal health coordinators at the Humana Cares main care center in St. Petersburg, Florida.

We restructured our benefits, and we deliberated as a senior executive team for the better part of a year on how best to do that. We conducted a value preference survey and asked our associates what their preferences would be.

—BONNIE HATHCOCK

SENIOR VICE PRESIDENT AND CHIEF HUMAN RESOURCES OFFICER

"That was a big piece of this. Just imagine the information flow that would be necessary in health care to get people engaged and empowered. It's crucial that the Internet be the core process for that."

SHIFTING HUMANA TO A CONSUMER-FOCUSED HEALTH BENEFITS COMPANY

In 2000, Humana was facing the same challenges as its customers—double-digit increases in health care costs. McCallister, who had recently become Humana's

CEO, was seeking an innovative solution to this dilemma and charged Bonnie C. Hathcock, Humana's senior vice president and chief human resources officer, with creating a new approach for the company's associates. Hathcock led a team that came up with a bold new strategy, one that would leverage an array of options, education, and information, and transform company associates from passive users into engaged consumers of health care.

"We restructured our benefits, and we deliberated as a senior executive team for the better part of a year on how best to do that. We conducted a value preference survey and asked our associates what their preferences would be," explained Hathcock.

The pilot program would serve as a laboratory and a showcase for Humana's future health care offerings to clients. "HR was handed a tall order—reform health care benefits for our company and for companies throughout the nation," Hathcock told *Human Resource Executive* magazine in a 2002 interview.

The result was a program called More Options and Choices for Humana Associates (MOCHA). The first version, unveiled in 2001 and called MOCHA 1, introduced consumer-directed health plans (CDHPs) along with traditional PPO and HMO plans. That first year, 6 percent of eligible associates chose the consumer-directed plans. Actuaries, accountants, and finance associates chose the CDHPs—they did the math. The first year, the MOCHA trend was 4.9 percent versus 19 percent for the market. Almost every plan saw positive behavior change. Communications, modeling tools, and associate feedback were critical in advancing the consumer strategy—and promoting change.

By MOCHA 10, the focus evolved to population health and overall well-being. The program featured

WORKPLACE WORKOUTS ///

Humana has often tested
its programs for health,
wellness, and consumer
empowerment with its own
associates, making for a
workplace that provides
plenty of opportunities
for healthy choices. Far
left: Michele Walker (right)
receives information from
Eric Feigl, an in-house
personal trainer at the
Cincinnati market office's
fitness center. Near left:
Account service executive
Toni Newton uses a weight
resistance machine at
Humana's Louisville
headquarters. Opposite:
Bonnie Hathcock, senior vice
president and chief human
resources officer, was named
Human Resource Executive
of the Year in 2007.

low-premium, high-deductible plans paired with tax-favored health savings accounts (HSAs). The MOCHA 10 plans also offered free preventive care and wellness initiatives aimed at effectively managing chronic illnesses and fostering positive behavior changes. In addition, Humana offered contributions to HSAs to offset a portion of the deductible, migrating to matching associate contributions on a sliding scale, based on salary. Through MOCHA, associates have become better-informed consumers, learning about health choices and finance, and the company and associates have both saved money.

"Normal insurance has a full deductible; auto insurance doesn't cover oil changes or door dings—but in health insurance it does," said Jim Bloem. "Everyone knows they have a health care liability, they just don't know how much it is, so they are afraid of taking a risk. They want full coverage and say, 'I'll pay for that.' What we've done with our own associates is show them how they can build assets to offset their liability. We showed people that if you want to raise deductibles, or reduce things that are covered instead of paying so much every pay period, you can pay a lot less and put the difference in a Health Savings Account. Once that's built up to $6,000 or $7,000, you can have a $3,000 deductible because now you have assets that counteract that unknown liability."

An important component of the consumer-focused health plan was a confidential health assessment questionnaire. The mandatory survey contained some thirty questions designed to help the firm identify potential health risks, and provided programs,

A NATIONAL TRAGEDY ///

Tom Noland, senior vice president of corporate communications, was in New York City with CEO Mike McCallister on September 11, 2001. The two were there with twenty-one other Humana team members to unveil the new Emphesys digital health plan. Top: Tom Noland in Louisville. Bottom: Tom Noland, Brian LeClaire, Bruce Goodman, Anthony Choate, Dr. Jack Lord, and Mike McCallister in New York City on September 11, holding the wet strips of torn tablecloth they used for facemasks during their walk out of the city after the World Trade Center towers collapsed.

incentives, and suggestions to those associates. In addition, to encourage associates to strive for better health, Humana offered financial incentives to those who participated in wellness programs. For example, they could earn up to $400 in gift cards for wearing a pedometer and reaching a designated number of miles. In 2008, Humana paid associates $1.1 million through this program. Associates could earn additional rewards by donating blood or participating in wellness web casts, and exchange them for fitness-oriented prizes such as gym memberships, running shoes, swimming lessons, and cookbooks. In 2008, associates won $976,000 in credits. Also, nonsmokers received a small discount on monthly premiums.

While Humana was busy rolling out its new associate health program, the Emphesys digital health plan was being prepared for a major national launch. The team streamlined its message of change, gathered testimonials, drilled the presentation, and assembled an invitation list of key media, Wall Street analysts, and other stakeholders for the event. Humana executives decided to travel to New York City to present this revolutionary digital health plan to the media and financial community. The company booked the Digital Sandbox, a high-tech event center at 55 Broad Street, just a block from the New York Stock Exchange. Invitations were sent out to Wall Street analysts and journalists that read "Change happens" followed by the launch date: September 11, 2001.

A twenty-three-member Humana team descended on lower Manhattan for the event, with half staying at the Marriott Financial Center Hotel, and the other half at the Marriott World Trade Center Hotel a block away. The logistical crew spent a long Monday, September 10, at the Digital Sandbox, setting up displays, systems, staging, lighting, projection screens, and live web feeds for the event. A Hollywood producer was hired to create a video backdrop evocative of Apple Inc.'s riveting "Tearing Down the Walls" campaign several years earlier—projected on a matrix of thirty-six televisions that formed a wall-size image. CEO Mike McCallister and two other executives went through several lengthy rehearsals, then headed to the Windows on the World restaurant, located on the 107th floor of the World Trade Center. They hosted a dinner for several dozen health policy leaders, large group employees, and technology VIPs—the last event ever hosted at the venue. One Humana team member had suggested a breakfast the next morning at the same location for guests who couldn't make the dinner, but was overruled. The decision saved dozens of lives.

Tuesday morning began with television interviews at Bloomberg Television in the American Stock Exchange for Mike McCallister and Tom Noland, senior vice president of corporate communications. The interview with a Bloomberg reporter ended at 8:44 a.m., two minutes before a Boeing 767 tore through the north tower of the World Trade Center between floors ninety-three and ninety-nine, just a half mile away. Outside, the two men could see the Trade Center, but not the side that had been struck by the plane; they were bewildered by a blizzard of falling paper, burning debris in the gutter, and the smell of airplane fuel. "At that point, our driver started shouting, 'It's a bomb! There's been a bomb!' and in no time the streets were gridlocked," McCallister told a reporter.

McCallister and Noland jumped out of the car and walked to 55 Broad Street, where they saw news coverage of the tragedy on the Digital Sandbox wall-size screen and began making calls to cancel Humana's event. When a second plane hit the South Tower, everyone realized the first crash wasn't an accident. The team hunkered down at 55 Broad Street, remaining

there as the first tower fell at 9:59 a.m. and the second at 10:28 a.m. "We were on the fourth floor and could look out the windows," McCallister recalled. "What was a bright, beautiful sunny day turned to black just like that. . . . It stayed dark outside our windows for nearly two hours."

Finally at 2:00 p.m., the group departed, using torn, wet strips of tablecloths for facemasks, walking through clouds of gray dust in an eerie quiet toward the East River before turning north. After walking thirty minutes, they encountered a Crystal Tours bus driver working on the engine of his sightseeing van in Chinatown and hired him to drive them to Harrisburg, Pennsylvania, where Humana arranged for a second bus to transport the group back to Louisville.

"The whole ordeal was something we'll never forget," McCallister said. "But it was nothing compared to what so many other people [were] going through—the victims, their families, and friends. We were just inconvenienced. Their lives have been torn apart. We were really very fortunate. And my heart goes out to everyone who was personally affected by this national tragedy." Humana published a book about the group's experience, with all proceeds going to charity.

EMPHESYS FORMS THE BACKBONE FOR NEW EMPLOYER PRODUCTS

When Emphesys was finally launched, it failed to gain traction with clients. "I think it was way too new, and the price points that were established were not sufficient to make people abandon their existing insurance plans," said Chief Operating Officer Jim Murray. But Humana took the information technology backbone created for Emphesys and integrated it with the plan designed for its own associates. The result was SmartSuite, which was offered to clients in 2002. The web-enabled, first-of-its-kind health benefits

Unless individuals have some knowledge of what things cost and what the options are, they make expensive choices. As there is more participation on the part of individuals in paying for their health care, an individual will choose—as in every other aspect of his or her life—the best value for their dollar.

—HEIDI MARGULIS
SENIOR VICE PRESIDENT, PUBLIC AFFAIRS

package allowed employers to select from one of four plan bundles, each containing up to six benefit plans. Associates would choose one of those plans, based on their health and budget needs, with the help of an online "Health Plan Wizard" that guided them through the plan option while ranking the plans based on the associates' preferences. The new products were designed so that consumers could choose the doctor, prescription drug, hospital, or treatment option they preferred, as long as they were willing to share a portion of the cost.

A year later, Humana released its next-generation product series, SmartSelect, which preserved the consumer-centric features of SmartSuite and also gave members the ability, through web-based tools, to customize health benefits for themselves and their families based on individual health histories, anticipated spending in the upcoming plan year, and their household budgets. Humana also launched HumanaOne, its first product designed for the individual health insurance market. SmartSelect allowed members to decide how to spend their health care dollars based on their preference for lower premiums/higher cost at point of service or higher premiums/lower cost at point of service. In 2004,

Humana brought its consumer-centric model to small business with the launch of SmartExpress, which offered many of the advantages that large employers typically enjoy, including a high-deductible health plan for individuals combined with the HSA funding mechanism.

Humana also began developing the informational tools needed to help members make better decisions. On Humana's web site, customers can plug in several dozen procedures that the insurer covers, choose potential hospitals or clinics, and then compare criteria, including cost, mortality figures, and number of procedures that institution has done in the last year—and then choose the facility that best meets their needs.

"When people are given options, they will generally choose a less invasive option," said Heidi Margulis, senior vice president, public affairs, who joined the company in 1985. "Some of the problems in the system have been caused by the fact that people have employer-based coverage and so they just spend on the employer's credit card. We have no idea what things cost; we think doctor's appointments are twenty dollars and prescription drugs are ten dollars. Unless individuals have some knowledge of what things cost and what the options are, they make expensive choices. As there is more participation on

the part of individuals in paying for their health care, an individual will choose—as in every other aspect of his or her life—the best value for their dollar."

Large employers quickly adopted Humana's revolutionary consumer-centric approach to health insurance. In 2002, just 2 percent of companies with one thousand employees or more offered the choice of a consumer-driven health plan. By 2010, the number of companies increased to 54 percent, according to a study published by Towers Watson and the National Business Group on Health. Moreover, research confirmed Humana's vision: placing consumers at the core of health care decision-making saves money and improves well-being. In July 2010, the Government Accountability Office (GAO) released a study examining the result of CDHPs. The GAO examined two large unidentified employers, one public and one private, that adopted a high-deductible health plan with a tax-advantaged account funded by the employer (also known as a health reimbursement arrangement, or HRA). On average, enrollees of both firms who chose those plans spent less and used fewer health care services

than those who remained in the PPO option, suggesting that the HRA groups were healthier.

Similarly, of the twenty-one studies GAO reviewed that assessed the health status of HRA and other CDHP enrollees, eighteen found they were healthier than traditional plan enrollees based on utilization of health care services, self-reported health status, or the prevalence of certain diseases or disease indicators. (The report noted that demographic factors may play a role, as policyholders in the HRA group were younger than those in the PPO group.)

Humana conducted its own four-year analysis of 231 companies and 219,000 Humana SmartSuite members from a range of industries. The study showed an annual medical cost trend in the 4- to 5-percent range—lower than the health care industry as a whole—as well as improved drug compliance rates and enhanced use of preventive health services, all with the employer/ employee cost share virtually unchanged.

REDEFINING MEDICARE

Along with its consumer-centered employer plans, Humana has applied the same philosophy to the biggest part of its business, private Medicare. It entered the arena in the mid-1980s and found its business transformed by the Medicare Modernization Act of 2003, the largest overhaul in the thirty-eight-year history of the program. The new law strengthened the traditional Medicare HMO product by offering subsidies to participating insurers, and allowed insurers to offer PPOs—the most popular form of health insurance in the U.S. at the time—more widely to senior citizens. The new law also introduced the Medicare Prescription Drug Plan (PDP), an entitlement benefit for prescription drugs. In 2006, Humana grew from $14 billion in annual revenues to $21 billion. By the year end, Humana had added nearly four million Medicare members.

MAKING SMART CHOICES ///

Informational tools like Humana SmartSelect allow members to make health care decisions that can save money as well as improve their well-being. Heidi Margulis, Humana's senior vice president, public affairs, left, believes that keeping consumers at the core of this decision-making process is key to controlling costs industry-wide.

ENSURING A SEAMLESS USER EXPERIENCE ///

As more members opt to access information about their plans through electronic means, Humana associates strive to make sure that the user experience is intuitive and engaging. Zahir Hussain Abdul-Salam (left) and Sameer Garg, associates working in information technology, discuss the consumer-facing system for the individual insurance product HumanaOne.

Among Humana's major innovations in the Medicare business has been the introduction of one-on-one interventions to keep seniors healthy and out of the hospital. For example, as early as 1997 Humana began studying its data and found that just five chronic medical conditions account for more than half of customers'—and thereby the company's—medical costs. Humana responded by introducing additional programs to help members manage these chronic conditions, including an intervention program to treat members suffering from congestive heart failure (CHF), a condition that affects 7 percent of older Americans.

By helping these members take better care of themselves, Humana reduced hospital costs associated with CHF by 78 percent in 1997, resulting in savings of $9 million. More important, the program reduced mortality among individuals with CHF from 25 percent to 10 percent and measurably increased activity levels, enabling these individuals to lead healthier lives.

In 1998, the company launched Humana Health Advanced Care Partners to help members with more than one disease or chronic condition to live healthier lives. For example, someone might be struggling with a combination of diabetes, cancer, heart disease, arthritis, sleep problems, or depression. Through this program, a Humana case manager works with the member and his primary care physician to develop an individualized care plan. Then, through frequent contact over the telephone and in person, the case manager monitors the member's compliance with the care plan and keeps the physician informed of the member's progress.

Humana piloted the program in Louisville, South Florida, Orlando, and Phoenix. The company's congestive heart failure initiative led to a 60 percent drop in hospital days and a 52 percent decrease in home health and other outpatient costs. Humana members affected by CHF showed an increased activity level of 15 percent. During 1998, the CHF program was featured in the peer-reviewed journal *Disease Management* and also was named a national exemplary practice program by the American Association of Health Plans.

Humana followed up with a similar program a decade later called Humana Cares, which looks more holistically at the challenges facing the company's neediest members—those with chronic conditions—to address both their medical and social needs. On average, each Humana Cares member sees fifteen different doctors and takes eleven prescription drugs. The goal is to bring more coordination to members' care and help with social and resource challenges.

"Humana Cares takes the most chronically ill patients and looks at them holistically and figures out how to make their life and health better," said Chris Todoroff, senior vice president and general counsel. "When we find certain seniors aren't doing as well with chronic conditions, we look for the root cause. Do they have someone to help get them to a grocery store? Does a community agency need to be contacted to deliver meals? Are they taking the prescriptions they are supposed to be taking? Are there safety issues? What can we do to offer a solution?"

Field managers visit members to check on these issues as well as to support and train caregivers who may be involved. The managers also assist the members with paperwork so prescriptions will be delivered regularly by mail, helping them to stay on a regimen and avoid acute episodes. In 2009, Humana Cares assessed 26,000 people. The program reduced hospitalization rates for the chronically ill by 36 percent and emergency room visits by 22 percent.

BRINGING IN THE PROFESSIONALS ///

Part of providing the best experience for customers meant providing the best available service. To that end, professional relations staff were dedicated to finding the country's best nurses and doctors for Humana hospitals. Far left: Professional nurse recruiters (from right) Margaret Nessen, Jo Ann Brent, Sandy Frederick, and an unidentified woman in 1977. Near left: Marilyn De Armas, a certified pharmacy technician at Prescribe It Rx, located within the Bird Road CAC-Florida Medical Center.

Richard Scherubel wrote to Humana about his experience in 2007: "Shortly after joining the PPO I was diagnosed with a chronic condition, for which I am being treated by a network dermatologist. To my great surprise, I was soon put in contact with a nurse who calls me quarterly to check on me, answer my questions, and who is available by phone 24/7. This is a welcome, free service provided through Humana for people with special conditions. I am also pleased to find that Humana provides coverage for the vision care services I need related to this condition. My annual medical premiums and co-pays were radically reduced from my previous insurance. And not only was I able to keep my doctor and hospital providers, but I have been able to find local specialists in the provider directory."

Overall, Humana's consumer-focused programs for Medicare members showed impressive results. In 2006, for example, the average Humana Medicare enrollee spent 1.6 days in the hospital, compared to 2.2 days for the average senior enrolled in original Medicare. The Humana member's average cost of care was $6,245—more than $1,000 less than the $7,458 spent on the average enrollee in original Medicare.

For chronically ill members, the results were even more dramatic. While an average original Medicare member with diabetes, heart failure, and Chronic Obstructive Pulmonary Disease spent 18.2 days in the hospital, his or her Humana counterpart was hospitalized for 10.7 days. The Humana member spent 3.9 days in a skilled nursing facility, compared to 14.2 days; had 11.7 home health visits, compared to 19.6; and had a cost of care of $24,978, compared to $43,589 for the original Medicare member. The figures were especially noteworthy at a time when evidence-based medicine was demonstrating that longer hospital stays do not automatically equate to better outcomes.

When people are hired they are instilled with the perfect service vision. We have yearly summits, we have monthly information and training programs, and we are very transparent with associates in talking with them about their individual engagement scores with the work team they are part of.

—JIM MURRAY
CHIEF OPERATING OFFICER

PERFECT SERVICE

While new Medicare enrollees praised Humana's service, the blistering pace of expansion put a strain on customer service in some of the company's other divisions. "We added four million new people to our rolls in one day, January 1, 2006," said COO Jim Murray. "January 1 is also the start of a lot of new effective dates for employer plans. As an organization we didn't do a good job of blocking and tackling and all the things necessary to deliver good service. We had two problems: the new Medicare enrollment and a lack of good basic service delivery. We were struggling mightily in the first months of 2006." Customer retention rates in some parts of the business plunged. For example, the small business division was losing seven thousand members a month. Humana hired Gallup to do an associate survey and found associates were only marginally engaged, invested, or even aware of ways the company could reach its goals. As more customers complained, associates became discouraged and complacent, and began to leave the company.

In July 2005, Mike McCallister commissioned a team of executives to launch a series of "Real World Work Sessions," asking the group to define what "perfect service" would look like for the firm's millions of customers. "We stepped back and decided we

won't let any roadblocks stand in the way. We asked each division to come back and give the company a guidebook to execute the concept of perfect service: not good, not world class, but perfect," said McCallister. "It says we have to look at every interaction, all the way from the point of sale to every piece of communication, the timing of how things work, and get away from the idea that service is something that happens down the street in the other building with people on the telephone. I don't want to compete against the other companies in our business—I want to compete against perfection. It was a great cultural siren song to the company to generate process improvement."

By the fall, the Real World Work group had come up with strategies to improve customer service interactions throughout the organization. In June 2006, Jim Murray and Bruce Goodman, senior vice president and chief information officer, gathered a group of 125 top executives at the Disney Institute in Orlando. "Disney personifies good service. That was the message we wanted to send: 'We want to be like Disney, like USAA, like Ritz Carlton,'" said Murray. "We took 125 folks and asked, 'What do you think about our service? How do you think we're doing?' We thought they might say, 'Service is fine—let's go on the rides.' But they said we were a 'D,' maybe an 'F,' in terms of service. For me that was a very key moment because people acknowledged we weren't where we needed to be. We began to create tactics and efforts to change our service delivery, but more importantly our service culture."

The Disney Institute guided the company leadership through lessons in quality, service, and loyalty. Although some leaders resisted the comparison between health insurance and entertainment, Disney's facilitators pointed out that both businesses were essentially commodities. The only way to distinguish them from competitors was through people, who provide outstanding customer service that generates repeat business. "We had to give people the tools to succeed and show them how their world fits into the overall vision of the company—how what one individual does every day links to what Humana is trying to accomplish—so there is a clear road map toward the company objective," said Murray. "Part of that is knowing what is expected of me when I walk in the door. We also focused on data and metrics that force us to ask why something occurs, and when we get the initial answer, ask why again. We continue to ask why until we understand the dynamics of the problem and how it can be solved."

Murray and Goodman met with ten thousand associates through a series of summits in 2006, introducing the concept of perfect service. Every customer service interaction had to meet a benchmark of six key characteristics: Accurate, Reliable, Easy to Use, Courteous, Proactive, and Personalized. Those goals were printed on cards and delivered to each associate. On the opposite side were the values that underlie perfect service: Integrity, Respect, Teamwork, Transparency, Accountability, Quality, Leadership, and Innovation. Associates were rewarded for their efforts in achieving perfect service and encouraged to come up

PRACTICE MAKES PERFECT SERVICE ///

In 2006, COO Jim Murray, left, and CIO Bruce Goodman met with ten thousand associates during a series of summits to introduce them to the key characteristics and values of perfect service. The result was a drop in call center volume, an increase in the company's small business division membership, and $50 million in savings.

with new approaches to old challenges. "When people are hired they are instilled with the perfect service vision," said Murray. "We have yearly summits, we have monthly information and training programs, and we are very transparent with associates in talking with them about their individual engagement scores with the work team they are part of."

The payoff for Humana has been significant. Following the work with the Disney Institute, Humana realized a $50 million savings thanks to improvements in customer service as well as reduced associate turnover rates. Associate engagement scores soared to the seventy-fifth percentile from the fiftieth percentile in just one year. The company's small business division began adding, rather than losing, seven thousand members a month. Call center volumes fell by 15 percent, or nearly two million calls. The company was ranked first in overall satisfaction in Texas and Ohio in a national health customer satisfaction study, and an audit declared Humana the best in the industry for claims resolution.

"You can't go anywhere in Humana without talking about perfect service," said Murray. "It's become part of our culture."

CONTINUING CARE ///

Humana has long understood the value of close ties between insurance providers and physicians in providing effective and affordable care to members. Far right: At the Bird Road CAC-Florida Medical Center in Miami, Florida, Ausberto Bianchi, MD, provides care to Angel Loriga. Near right: Medical assistants Melba Monje (seated) and Niola Yero review patient records.

BACK TO THE FUTURE: CLOSER TIES BETWEEN INSURANCE AND PHYSICIANS

In recent years, Humana has accelerated its transformation into a more integrated, consumer-focused benefit provider through a series of acquisitions. They include CompBenefits Corporation, a nationwide dental and vision company, and KMG America Corporation, which specializes in employer-sponsored voluntary benefits. Perhaps most significant, in December 2010 Humana completed its acquisition of Concentra, a privately held Texas health care company, for $790 million in cash. Through its affiliated clinicians, Concentra delivers occupational medicine, urgent care, physical therapy, and wellness services to members and the general public from more than three hundred medical centers in forty-two states. Nearly three million Humana medical members live near a Concentra center. In addition to its medical center locations, Concentra serves employer customers by providing a broad range of health advisory services and operating more than 240 work site medical facilities.

"We continue to grow on the physician side, building tighter and tighter relations with the physicians we do business with," said Tom Liston, senior vice president, senior products. "We will continue to acquire or invest in companies that manage them. The reason that's so important is because consumers today don't generally rate their experience with the health care system very highly. People don't know how to navigate the system when they get sick; they feel like they have to jump through a lot of hoops. To the extent we can integrate with the front line services that are delivering care, we can help create an experience that's more logical and meaningful to the member."

Although a conflict of interest between hospitals and health insurance led Humana to split into two separate companies in 1993, Paul Kusserow, senior vice president and chief strategy officer, said there's a big difference this time around, especially as consumers are more focused on getting value for their health care dollars. "We used to simply sell health insurance to members. Now we're figuring out what their needs are

> The business strategy is to improve well-being and provide good health care through diversified services. We've owned hospitals in the past, but Concentra helps keep people out of hospitals.
>
> **—PAUL KUSSEROW**
> SENIOR VICE PRESIDENT AND CHIEF STRATEGY OFFICER

and supplying a continuum of different products so they'll stay with us," he explained. "The business strategy is to improve well-being and provide good health care through diversified services. We've owned hospitals in the past, but Concentra helps keep people out of hospitals. As technology increases, as you can do more things on an outpatient basis, you can have better recovery times and fewer issues with infection. Concentra allows for alternative site care so a procedure or treatment can be done outside the hospital more safely, more effectively, with lower cost and an equally successful outcome."

Along with forging closer ties with physicians, Humana is working on a pilot program to develop physician incentives that would improve the quality of care. In fall 2010, Humana was selected to be a federal accountable care organization (ACO) pilot program, one of only five nationally, in partnership with a Louisville hospital. The ACOs are charged with developing new financial incentives for care providers based on good health outcomes rather than volumes of procedures done. This would increase quality and efficiency, better coordinate patient care, eliminate waste, and reduce the overuse and misuse of care.

For Humana, it's a refinement of a model it pursued in the 1980s. "At one time the company was big into integration and big in the provider space and then we got out of it completely. There was a conflict of interest between being a finance entity and a provider of the services, and I don't think the marketplace was ready for it," said McCallister. "We are taking a step back into the future in having physicians become part of our organization, but it will look different from the HMO of the 1980s. Doctors are selling their practices to hospitals left and right, and moving away from owning small businesses because it's complicated and difficult, and many just want to see patients. It's a big movement for doctors to be in something like Concentra. As part of improving health care, we need to have a close, tight relationship with the doctors to get the quality up and to meet metrics around performance. We have to start gluing the system together rather than hope doctors will get to the right level of service. We are a huge organization with a lot of physicians and a lot of locations, and to get close to us in terms of performance, they need to be partners."

03

—

AN EVOLVING MISSION

CONFIDENT OPTIMISM ///

Humana founders Wendell Cherry and David A. Jones in front of Heritage House, their first nursing home. The spirit of optimism that led the two to invest in a nursing home would continue to drive Humana's growth with new visions and new markets.

AS HUMANA HAS DEVELOPED THROUGH THE YEARS, THE TRUTH IS THAT WE HAVE ALWAYS BEEN INVOLVED IN HELPING PEOPLE. WE HAVE ALWAYS HAD A DIRECT CONNECTION TO INDIVIDUALS' HEALTH AND WELL-BEING.

—MIKE MCCALLISTER
CHAIRMAN AND CHIEF EXECUTIVE OFFICER

SHARED EXPERTISE ///

As Humana's business model has changed, it has maintained a consistent connection to understanding the clinical aspects of its business practices. Frederik Tomlin (facing), market vice president and medical officer for the commercial team based in Chicago, speaks to Jon Harts, the group's director of commercial sales.

SERIOUS BUSINESS ///
Humana quickly evolved
from a two-man operation
to the largest nursing home
company in the country.
Cherry and Jones, circa 1973,
with Bill Young, director
(seated left), and Humana
officers (left to right) Carl
Pollard, Bill Ballard, Joe
Greene, and Lin McLellan.

Humana's goal of improving health care delivery is just the most recent interpretation of a value that lies deep in the company's roots: the desire to be the best. For a half century, Humana has demonstrated its ambition to find the best opportunities; to build products and services that best serve the customers' needs; and to create an environment that allows associates to do their best work. The ambition to be the best built a Fortune 100 company. But first, it built a nursing home.

The seeds for what would become a $34 billion company were planted in the summer of 1961, during a chance encounter between cofounder David A. Jones and a high school acquaintance, Brian McCoy. Jones had been assigned to help sell the homes of the executives with the Reynolds Metals Company, which relocated to Richmond, Virginia, in 1958 after being denied zoning approval to build new headquarters in the Louisville suburbs. McCoy showed up to make an offer on the luxury home of the Reynolds CEO. "Brian, like me, had grown up in humble circumstances in Louisville," Jones recalled. "I asked him how he was able to make an offer on such an expensive home, and he said, 'Dave, last year I built a nursing home.'"

McCoy had developed the Twinbrook Nursing Home on Dutchmans Lane in Louisville, which opened in 1960 to great success. "When I saw how well Brian was doing with his nursing home investment, I rushed back to the office and said, 'Wendell, let's build a nursing home.' That was all the market research we did. We jumped into it with the confidence of total ignorance. We knew nothing about nursing homes, but I saw this guy who opened a nursing home the year before and was already buying the most expensive home in Louisville." On August 18, 1961, Jones and Cherry formed a company called WenDav Inc., a name soon changed to Heritage House Nursing and Convalescent Care, Inc.

By the early 1960s, professional nursing homes were still relatively rare. At the turn of the century, with no federal assistance available, most states housed their poorest citizens in "poor farms" or "almshouses"—typically rundown facilities offering minimal care. A few religious and immigrant communities established services for the impoverished and elderly, but these hardly met the need. In 1935, the Social Security Act became law and provided states with matching grants for old-age benefits to retired workers.

In order to discourage the growth of public almshouses, however, federal matching funds were restricted to people living in private facilities. That opened the door to a variety of private old-age homes. But many of them were converted, old multistory houses that posed difficulties—and danger in the event of fire—for frail, bedridden, and wheelchair-bound residents.

In the 1950s, the Social Security Act was amended to require states to begin licensing nursing homes, and the ban on federal benefits to residents of public facilities was removed. In an effort to improve the quality of care, a separate 1954 law offered grants for the construction of nursing homes in conjunction with hospitals, and professional facilities began to emerge.

a wonderful new concept in
NURSING *and*
CONVALESCENT CARE
Heritage House
"their home away from home"
3535 Bardstown Road
Corner of Liverpool Lane

ASSEMBLING A TEAM

Jones and Cherry had bold ambitions but little capital, so they chose to lease rather than buy the land for the project. They approached Lewis "Sonny" Bass and Charles L. Weisberg, cousins and Wyatt clients who owned the real estate firm Bass & Weisberg. They became partners and immediately went in search of a suitable site. Contractors Bill Rommel and Jim McFerran agreed to build the nursing home without any profit or overhead in return for the opportunity to purchase one-third of the stock. Each of the six partners invested $1,000. (Cherry came up with his portion by floating a second loan on his 1960 Valiant; Jones secured his from the Household Finance Corporation) Jones provided the legal and accounting work.

The team hired an architect to design a seventy-eight-bed nursing home for the two-acre site. The single-story, H-shaped facility had a nursing station at the end of each corridor so attendants could keep an eye on most of the rooms. The large center section held a dining room and a common area featuring a piano, where activities and entertainment were organized for residents and guests. The partners' wives decorated the lobby, dining room, and other areas of the facility. "This nursing home was to be a new kind of nursing home . . . more like a hospital—bright and clean," Bass noted. "We had a vision that we felt was greatly needed."

Next, Jones approached Charlie Will, the president of Portland Federal Savings and Loan Association, and negotiated a loan for 80 percent of the land value and projected cost. They persuaded mechanical contractor Jack Zender to install $100,000 in plumbing, heating, and air conditioning equipment in exchange for a five-year promissory note at 9 percent interest. "Putting those sources together enabled us to build the nursing home with a little cash left over for working

capital," Jones recalled. "My wife, Betty, used to worry sometimes about the amount of debt we'd taken on. It was a reflection of my optimistic attitude that I told her she didn't need to worry about that—the banks needed to worry about that."

The partners bought all the equipment from American Hospital Supply. The firm's "ambitious and extremely optimistic salesman" promised everything would be delivered and assembled in time for the grand opening on August 10, 1962, Jones recalled. In fact, much of the furniture didn't arrive until August 9. "We stayed up all night, Wendell and I, our partners and all our wives, putting together the furniture, including the bed

springs, which in those days were made of metal that had to be connected," Jones said. "We all had cut fingers and were pretty tired by our grand opening on the morning of the 10th of August."

Finally, they discussed potential names for the nursing home. "We had decided to call it Hermitage House after President Jackson's home in Nashville, Tennessee," Jones recalled. "We hired a talented young artist, Keith Spears, who has become quite successful, to draw a logo. He misspelled the name, leaving out the 'm,' so it turned into Heritage House. We couldn't afford to have it done again, so that's how we got our name." The young partners celebrated the facility's completion with

a spaghetti dinner and wine served by Caesar Bertoli, who had done tile and masonry work for the home. "He was a great big powerful man; he had a great voice, and he loved to imitate [Italian tenor Enrico] Caruso," Jones recalled. "He was also a splendid cook."

The first day of operations, the exhausted team was ready to receive patients. But their inaugural guest was a completely unexpected patient: the administrator they hired to run the facility, a nurse named Stella Stoll, who had become ill. "She was a truly wonderful, lovely woman who had been very helpful to us in the planning stages and in getting everything ready," said Jones. "But when we were about to receive patients she got ill and became our very first patient."

Management of the facility fell back on Jones and Cherry. Luckily, Stoll had hired a few nurses, and ten patients were scheduled to arrive. "The semi-private rates were eleven dollars per night, and privates were twenty dollars per night. Those rates seem pretty quaint today," said Jones. "We succeeded in opening the nursing home, but it was a struggle without a competent, full-time administrator."

Jones recruited an old friend, Elmer Shaffner, to become the full-time administrator. "Elmer and I had worked together for a couple of summers while I was in law school at the accounting firm of Irvin L. Wasserman and Associates," Jones recalled. Shaffner had left the company to become an assistant administrator of Our Lady of Peace Hospital in Louisville. "He'd had that job for only a couple of years, but he had a whole lot more experience than either Wendell or I," said Jones. "We hired Elmer, and he brought professionalism to the nursing home. That was one of the wisest moves we ever made. His salary was a slight burden at the beginning, but he relieved the pressure on the two of us. He hired good people for the laundry, for food service, for various

therapies that were involved in the nursing home, and before long it was running smoothly." Shaffner eventually became vice president and director of the eastern division of nursing centers.

EXPANSION INTO LEXINGTON AND BEYOND _____

With the nursing home providing a much-needed modern facility to the Louisville community, the partners soon sought to duplicate their success. Sonny Bass introduced them to a friend, Dr. Maury Kauffman, who had identified a similar demand for a nursing home in nearby Lexington. "Maury helped us put together a group of doctors and other investors to raise the $100,000 needed," Bass related. The partners formed a new company to develop the project, with local investors loaning $100,000 to the corporation, plus $5,000 for half of the common stock, and the original partners investing $5,000 for the other half of the stock.

The 120-bed Lexington facility opened in 1964. "It was an instant success, in part because of the physician-investors who let it be known throughout the medical community that Lexington now had a first-class, newly constructed nursing home," said Jones.

Two Lexington investors would become crucial to the young company's growth and success: Hilary J. Boone, Jr., and John W. Landrum. Boone, a general agent for the Massachusetts Mutual Life Insurance Company, offered to help the nascent firm find investor groups in other cities through his MassMutual colleagues and quickly assembled partnerships in New Haven and Waterbury, Connecticut. Landrum joined the board of directors, on which he served until 1993.

With successful facilities in Kentucky and Connecticut, the partners looked further afield. They found a real estate broker who was traversing the Southeast seeking new sites for Thornton's Inc.

A SECOND HOME ///

After the success of the first nursing home in Louisville, and recognizing the demand for a similar home in Lexington, the partners decided to open a second home to meet the needs of the Lexington community. With the help of local physicians and investors, the Lexington home quickly proved successful. Far left: The partners' second nursing home, which opened in Lexington in 1964. Near left: Cherry and Jones with Elmer Shaffner (center) in 1971, at the tenth anniversary of the company's founding.

to build gas stations. They hired him to investigate possible nursing home acquisitions. He promptly identified a facility in Virginia Beach, Virginia, owned by the manager, George Holmes. But financing was complicated, and the partners nearly lost the deal. "George Holmes promised orally to provide a $35,000 second mortgage loan, and we were able to obtain a first mortgage loan to pay the balance of the purchase price," Jones recalled. "As the time neared for the closing on that acquisition, George received a better offer for the nursing home. He waited until the evening before the scheduled closing and called to tell us that he would not lend us the promised $35,000, leaving us in a very difficult position." Unless the partners could come up with $35,000 cash, they weren't going to be able to acquire the nursing home.

But Jones and Cherry were a resourceful pair. "At that point, I called a good friend—Sam Klein, president and chief executive officer of the Bank of Louisville, who turned out to be a saint—and told him of my dilemma,"

Jones explained. "He said, 'Dave, prepare a note and have all six partners sign it as guarantors, and bring it down to the bank, and I'll open the bank and give you a certified check for $35,000 in return for your promissory note signed by the six partners.' So that very evening I met Sam at the bank on the corner of 4th and Market Streets in Louisville. He brought his nephew, Bertram Klein, who knew how to operate the certified check machine." The partners delivered the certified check, along with the first mortgage loan at the closing the next day.

George Holmes graciously accepted the unexpected outcome and stayed on as administrator of the nursing home. "We learned a phenomenal amount from him," said Jones. "He turned out to be an exceptional manager who kept the home clean; he personally supervised the preparation of all the food; he knew every patient in the facility by name. He knew their family members. He was kind to everyone, and he created an atmosphere of caring and compassion that set a standard for our young but fast-growing organization."

Each of us owned a different percentage. The critical issue was to gain everyone's agreement on what their respective values were. As one can imagine, that was a very, very difficult negotiation. I believe it to be the single most important negotiation in the history of Humana.

—DAVID A. JONES

COFOUNDER

A CRITICAL NEGOTIATION

By 1964, the partners' situation had become complex. Jones and Cherry had purchased the interests of Bill Rommel and Jim McFerran for $128,000. Now, four of the original six partners owned the Louisville nursing home as well as one-half interest in the nursing home in Lexington, Kentucky. Three other investor groups were involved in the properties in Lexington, New Haven, and Waterbury. "Each of us owned a different percentage," said Jones. "The critical issue was to gain everyone's agreement on what their respective values were. As one can imagine, that was a very, very difficult negotiation. I believe it to be the single most important negotiation in the history of Humana."

Jones directed the negotiations and secured agreement from everyone except a lawyer named Nathan Elliot. Jones recalled, "He told his Lexington investor partners that 'before long, Jones is going to leave the law practice and become the chief executive officer, with a salary of $150,000 per year; Cherry's going to join him as number two for $100,000; and Hilary Boone, your colleague over here, is going to become secretary of the corporation at $50,000 per year.' Now my salary at that time was about $15,000 a year, so those were big, big numbers. Hilary Boone stood up and said, 'Nathan,

if you're not interested in going along, I will buy you out.' And Nathan said, 'done.' So Hilary Boone bought Nathan Elliott's share and our negotiation was complete! Each 5 percent share in the Lexington nursing home ultimately became worth more than $30 million, so Hilary Boone did well by his unwavering belief in me."

The result of the 1964 negotiations was a single corporation, called Heritage House of America. The forty investors who had owned an interest in a single nursing home now held stock in a company that owned all the nursing homes. Boone, Landrum, Bass, Weisberg, Cherry, and Jones formed the board of directors.

Heritage House immediately looked for capital to grow, seeking a $500,000 loan from Marine Midland Bank. The bank had a small business investment corporation, allowing it to make loans with risks shared partly by the federal government. But interest rates were high and the bank required a substantial equity opportunity. Boone recommended that the company approach William T. Young, a Lexington businessman who had considered the second nursing home deal but decided to pass.

Young had majored in engineering at the University of Kentucky, graduating in 1939. He served in the U.S. Army during the war and married his college sweetheart, Lucy Maddox. Lucy's father owned a peanut processing company, and in 1946 she and Bill started the Big Top Peanut Butter Company. The couple put jars of peanut butter in the trunk of Young's Chevrolet coupe and drove all around the country, calling on chain stores and mom-and-pop outlets, creating a distribution network. Lucy, an art school graduate, created unique designs that were etched onto the glass jars; when the top was removed, the empty jar could be used as a drinking glass. Every few months, Lucy produced new designs, and collectors began snapping them up. In 1955, Bill and Lucy sold Big Top Peanut Butter to Procter & Gamble, which changed the company name to "Jif." Young bought a controlling interest in RC Cola Company and became its non-executive chairman.

Young agreed to loan Heritage House $500,000 at a lower interest rate than the bank, subordinate to all other debt, in exchange for warrants to acquire common stock. He joined the board, insisting that Jones leave the Wyatt law practice and become chairman and chief executive officer of the nursing home company. "When I met Bill in 1965, he was one of the wealthiest people in Lexington," Jones recalled. "He was a sagacious, successful entrepreneur who had built his own company, with wide distribution and unique characteristics. He sold it for a good price and had purchased a controlling interest in a sleepy old cola company in Columbus, Georgia, that sold branded products. He was a great addition to our board, bringing experience, judgment, and mature insights along with his money."

With the capital infusion from Young, Heritage House grew to eight nursing homes by mid-1967, with plans for more. Revenues rose to $2 million, with profits of about $150,000. Jones started his own law firm because two of his clients, a manufacturer and a real estate developer, had asked if they could continue with him when he left Wyatt. "Suddenly I was busy as a

CAPITAL GROWTH ///

In the mid-1960s, Heritage House began seeking capital to continue the corporation's growth. They turned to Bill Young, a Lexington entrepreneur who made his fortune after starting the Big Top Peanut Butter Company in 1946—later known as the popular brand Jif. Young agreed to loan Heritage House $500,000, which they used to grow to eight nursing homes by 1967. Left: Young (right) and David Scott, a member of the board of directors from 1974 to 1990, at a meeting in the late 1980s.

lawyer but still had plenty of free time to devote to the growth of Heritage House," he said. Cherry joined him in February 1967, and the law firm became Jones and Cherry. Cherry would also lead construction activities for the firm that eventually became Humana—a role he continued to play until his untimely death from cancer at age fifty-five in 1991.

A HOT PUBLIC OFFERING

In the fall of 1967, Pye Conway, a stockbroker at Stein Bros. & Boyce who knew Jones, asked if he would like to take the company public. "I thought that was strange as we still were a very small company," said Jones.

HUMANA /// TODAY

**BRINGING ISSUES
TO LIGHT ///**

Weekly one-on-one
meetings allow Humana
directors the opportunity
to provide personal
guidance to their own
team members. Dave
Lewis (left), director of
financial operations for
Humana's innovation and
marketing organization,
receives an update from
financial operations
consultant Craig Domeck.

"But Pye replied that one nursing home company had already come public, and he knew of several others that were in the pipeline, so I agreed to take a look."

Cherry, Jones, and Conway flew to New York to meet I. W. "Tubby" Burnham II, who had founded Burnham & Company in the midst of the Depression with a $100,000 loan from his grandfather and ultimately turned it into the fifth largest investment bank on Wall Street.

Heritage House's audit was conducted by a young partner at local accounting firm Yeager, Ford & Warren named Carl Pollard. Burnham urged Jones and Cherry to discharge the local firm and hire a national one in preparation for the IPO. Jones refused, telling Burnham that if he wasn't willing to take the firm public using Yeager, Ford & Warren that he would find another investment banker. Burnham reluctantly conceded.

"One of the reasons that Mr. Burnham may have had some concern about Carl Pollard was that when they first met, Carl was wearing a sport coat, at a time when most people on Wall Street wore blue suits or gray suits," Jones recalled. "Carl's sport coat was quite spectacular, probably the prettiest one ever sold in his hometown of Lancaster, Kentucky. It was a combination of red and purple, and was quite a sight to see, especially on Wall Street." Pollard agreed to buy a gray suit.

Heritage House offered a 25 percent stake in the firm—250,000 shares—priced at eight dollars per share, expecting to raise $2 million in capital. (The original investors owned the other 750,000 shares.) The stock opened on January 31, 1968, at double the offering price and ended the day around twenty dollars. "That indicated to Wendell and me that the stock had been underpriced by Burnham, but they argued that it was a function of the fact that nursing home companies were very much in demand at that moment," Jones said. "So we were

unhappy that we had sold at too low a price, and ecstatic at the value of our company and of our shares."

The stock continued to rise throughout 1968, reaching a high of eighty-four dollars per share in December, when it split two-for-one. The firm launched a follow-on offering, raising $11.6 million, as well as another $7 million in a 6 percent convertible subordinated debenture, so it had more than $18 million in cash to fuel growth. Heritage House had begun the fiscal year with seven nursing homes containing 911 beds. A year later, the company had grown four-fold, with 4,025 beds in thirty-four centers in twelve states in operation, under construction, or in acquisition agreement. Revenues rose to $4.8 million in 1968 from $3 million in 1967, and earnings after tax increased 86 percent to $316,000.

By the end of 1969, the chain comprised fifty nursing homes in the U.S., making it the largest operator in the country, and had completed or nearly completed ten additional homes in Canada. On July 2, 1969, the firm was listed on the American Stock Exchange.

GOING PUBLIC ///

In 1967, Heritage House, still a small company, became one of several nursing home corporations to be taken public. Their initial public offering was for 250,000 shares, a 25 percent stake in the company. The shares were priced at eight dollars each, but when the stock hit the market on January 31, 1968, it opened at double that and closed around twenty dollars a share. Left: Celebrating Heritage House's IPO at the Waldorf Astoria, January 31, 1968. Opposite: Jones (middle) and David Grissom (second from right) with representatives at the New York Stock Exchange in 1971.

Revenues for the fiscal year jumped to $17.7 million from $7.7 million, and net income more than doubled to $1.1 million.

A year later Heritage House changed its name to Extendicare to more closely reflect the nature of its business. But the stock frenzy that had fueled its growth coincided with the tail end of a roaring bull market and the beginning of difficult economic times in the country as a whole. Over the next six years, Extendicare's stock would decline to $7.50 per share. Some eighty-three nursing home operators had gone public in the second half of the 1960s, following the enactment of the new Medicare law on July 1, 1966. "We weren't feeling the positive effects of Medicare to any great extent at that time, and our growth plans were formulated without regard to Medicare," said Jones. "Nonetheless, it was a driver of our stock price until people realized that it wasn't such a bonanza for nursing home companies."

Recognizing that the need for modern nursing homes was being quickly met, Extendicare's executives considered other opportunities. "We asked ourselves what it was that we knew how to do," recalled Jones. "We decided that we were good at raising money, and we were good at obtaining needed zoning by convincing neighbors to allow us to build something in a neighborhood that they probably really didn't want—a nursing home. We asked ourselves what else is like that, and answered, 'trailer parks' or mobile home parks."

David Grissom had just joined the company in 1969 from the Wyatt law firm as an executive vice president and board member. He took on the charge to build the mobile home business, and within one year, Extendicare expanded from a single park with ninety-two spaces and four retail outlets to eleven mobile home parks containing 1,628 spaces and twenty-three retail outlets. Heritage House would buy a park, rent out the spaces, and sell

the mobile homes to fill them. The interest rate to buyers of the trailers was about 14 percent, and the seller was required to cosign the borrower's loan. As a result, when a loan went bad, Extendicare ended up paying the 14 percent interest. Ironically, the company could access capital at 6 percent.

"We could have borrowed the money ourselves at 6 percent, and loaned it to the borrower and made the 8 percent spread," Jones explained. "The mobile home park business was a disaster, and we were properly humbled. During the next fiscal year, we made one of the smartest moves in the history of our company. We shut down the mobile home business, absorbed our significant losses, learned a lesson about sticking to what we understood, and concentrated on our health care business, which was prospering." Net income in fiscal 1971 fell by nearly half, to $1.6 million, even as revenues increased 62 percent, to $86.7 million.

The mobile home parks fiasco played an important role in future success, Jones said. "I suspect that our early and continuing success had led to a bit of hubris, and as with the Greek gods, we were severely punished and chastened," he explained. "That lesson, however, has proven to be worth its weight in gold. We shut it down, took our losses, and moved in a new direction. While we were then, and continue to be, action-oriented, our future actions were much more thoughtful. We also learned that when you bring a weak or bad asset onto the balance sheet, it ultimately has to depart through the income statement. The result of that lesson is that Humana has never allowed a time bomb on its balance sheet. It has no unfunded liabilities for pension or health care or other promises whose future costs cannot be foreseen."

A NEW ERA

Fortunately, Extendicare had looked at another avenue for diversifying its business. In 1968, Extendicare agreed to lease Medical Center Hospital, a 305-bed facility under construction in Huntsville, Alabama. A year later, the firm acquired four small hospitals and one large new facility then under construction.

Hospitals were a natural extension of the health care mission and skills Extendicare had developed in operating nursing homes, and the company spied an opportunity to bring professional management and customer service to an industry that lacked both. As the company noted in its 1969 annual report: "Extendicare believes its management techniques will make it possible for hospitals to reduce their expenses. The savings can be used to halt the spiral of rate increases, to improve the quality of patient care where possible, and to produce a satisfactory profit."

Moreover, revenues were significantly higher in hospitals than in nursing homes. In 1970, attorney

William Ballard, Jr., joined the firm as executive vice president and chief financial officer. "I could tell you we did a wonderful business plan, and we really thought about it and did a pro forma—but none of that would be true," said Ballard. "In those days you were paid $15 to $20 a day for a bed in a nursing home, and hospitals were paid $100 to $120 a day."

The move into hospitals came out of an experience with the company's New Haven nursing home, Jones said. "Connecticut had a bad flu season in 1966 and the hospitals in New Haven filled up, so we began to admit elderly patients directly to our nursing home," he recalled. "The Medicare law came into effect in July, and that was a source of payment for people over sixty-five. We were able to provide the care they would have gotten at the hospital, as long as they didn't need surgery, but the hospital was paid ten times as much per day as we were. A light bulb went off in my head, and I decided we should be in that business, because we knew at least half of what was needed to care for patients. I would say we acted in total ignorance—as we had when we built the first nursing home. But Wendell and I were both focused and passionate about what we were doing, so we pitched in and learned that business."

Rosanne Miller, who served as executive secretary to Jones, said the founders had a sense of humor about their willingness to learn along the way as they entered a new business: "We have a poster in the office from the company's twenty-fifth anniversary with caricatures of Mr. Jones and Mr. Cherry and a sentence written in Latin that means 'in ignorance there is hope.'"

During difficult economic times, and after the "disaster" of the mobile home parks investment, Extendicare diversified its business by taking on Medical Center Hospital in Huntsville, Alabama, in 1968. As with their initial investment in nursing homes, the founders of Extendicare had little experience running hospitals, but they believed the skills they learned from their nursing homes could be translated to hospitals, and their success proved them right. By the end of 1970, Extendicare operated twenty-one hospitals. Below: An Extendicare newsletter from 1972. Opposite: David Grissom, who joined Extendicare in 1969 as an executive vice president and board member.

LOURDES HALL

ST. JOSEPH'S INFIRMARY — LOUISVILLE, KY.

Extendicare moved decisively and aggressively, and in just twelve months, hospitals accounted for the majority of its business. "Almost every development project we investigate is the result of an invitation from the community or some segment to build a hospital there," Jones told *Louisville Magazine* in an interview in 1971. "We get two to three inquiries every week from communities that want new hospitals."

By the end of fiscal 1970, Extendicare had opened or acquired twenty-one hospitals with 2,162 beds, including Kentucky's largest hospital, the 507-bed St. Joseph's Infirmary in Louisville. On the nursing home side, Extendicare grew to forty-eight centers with 5,954 beds. Revenues rocketed from $30 million to $60 million, and net income roughly doubled to $3.1 million. William Barnhart, Jr., who served as executive director of the original Alabama hospital, was promoted to vice president and director of hospitals.

By the end of fiscal 1971, Extendicare had become the third largest for-profit hospital management company in the U.S. and was listed on the New York Stock Exchange. It owned thirty-eight facilities containing 3,207 beds.

A QUICK EXIT, AND SWIFT GROWTH

In 1972, Extendicare faced a financial challenge in its nursing home business, prompted by a regulatory change in California. "We had sixteen or seventeen nursing homes in California, and the state's MediCal program gave nursing home providers fourteen dollars a day for taking care of patients," explained Pollard. "Three-quarters of our patients were on MediCal. The new governor, Ronald Reagan, slashed rates by 10 percent and eliminated our

margin of profit entirely. With that, we decided to try to sell the California homes."

Pollard took on the assignment and traveled to Milwaukee to see a competitor, National Health Enterprises. "The CEO said, 'We'll buy California if you sell us all of [your nursing homes].' I said okay and cut the deal. I came home, and I don't think David and Wendell were very happy. We wanted to exit California, but I don't know that they were quite as ready to completely exit the business. But we got them sold. That was our exit from the nursing home business, and it virtually happened overnight."

On September 1, 1972, Extendicare sold its interest in forty-one nursing homes for $14 million in cash and notes, and received an acute-care hospital from National Health Enterprises. Extendicare retained four nursing centers that were integral to hospitals the company owned. "All of us at Extendicare consider it a privilege to be on the leading edge of a new idea—that investor-owned corporations can meet the hospital care needs of the American people in a way that offers distinct advantages to everyone concerned," Jones wrote in his 1972 letter to stockholders.

In January 1974, the company decided to change its name to better reflect its mission and distance itself from its nursing home connotation. It hired the corporate identity firm Lippincott & Margulies, which produced a list of five hundred names. "The names fell into three categories: bridge names with some link to the previous name; descriptive names from words descriptive of a business; and coined names that were invented words," recalled Charlie Teeple, former vice president of investor relations and communications. "Management went through the list, discarding name after name until only a few remained. Chosen to replace Extendicare was a coined name, Humana."

THE HUMANA SYSTEM

The company formalized its health care improvement strategy under the name the "Humana System." The starting point "was an understanding of people who use hospitals—the customers," the 1975 annual report explained. "In-depth research on the values, expectations, and attitudes of patients and physicians was undertaken. . . . Knowledge thus gained was utilized by Humana associates in developing procedures and standards that give strong consideration to customer preferences.

Humana believes that, by considering patients and doctors as customers and by offering services responsive to their values, an enhanced level of satisfaction with hospital care can be achieved."

The Humana System's measuring and monitoring of quality surpassed the accreditation requirements of the Joint Commission on Accreditation of Hospitals. Rather than dictate standards, Humana engaged hospital staff in both the evaluation and setting of measurable criteria.

THE PRESCRIPTION FOR STRONG SERVICE ///

Members who use Humana's RightSource mail order pharmacy service can receive personal guidance from pharmacists and technicians for any of their questions or concerns— just like in a bricks-and-mortar pharmacy. Steve Poignon (standing), a pharmacist who serves as manager of member services at the West Chester, Ohio, facility, speaks to front-line leaders Meredith Winter (left) and Patricia Keller.

"We believe that jobs should be meaningful, with resulting employee satisfaction and productivity," the 1975 annual report stated. "As the standards for each process are determined and documented, each employee is trained and motivated toward the achievement of those standards. Continuous training leads to consistent performance." Humana's education department developed programs to teach technical skills that incorporated the values and needs identified in the customer research at all levels of the company.

In every hospital, Jones and Cherry also set up a local board, which included people elected by their peers in every department of major services, such as pediatrics, surgery, and obstetrics-gynecology. "They were amazed; they had never been invited to join a board," Jones recalled. "But no one knew more about the hospital than they did. They took ownership of the hospital and were tremendous advocates. To me it was a simple idea of being inclusive, but for the hospitals we acquired it was revolutionary."

Excellent training and a strong sense of engagement and purpose led Humana to industry-leading productivity. While every industry in the U.S. economy enjoyed productivity growth in the post-war period, average hospital productivity declined between 1946 and 1973. Over that period, the number of hospital workers per patient increased from 1.48 to 3.15, according to the American Hospital Association. "By improved training and better organization of the necessary tasks, Humana is now providing an improved level of service quality with only 2.2 employees per patient," compared with 3.2 in similar hospitals, the 1975 annual report noted.

As a result, Humana's associates gained an appreciation for how their tasks contributed to the care of patients and larger success of the company.

David Campisano started working in hospital billing in 1969 out of high school and stayed with the company as he finished college, recently celebrating his fortieth anniversary. "As I worked with the information in front of me, I became very interested in how all the data fit together, how patients interacted with the medical staff, how that applied to billing and special projects—and began to see how important it was for the information and services to be available for people," he recalled. "I thought, 'I need to do a good job so I can keep this process going.'"

STANDARDIZING SYSTEMS

From the beginning, Humana centralized purchasing and billing to reduce costs and improve economies of scale. The firm introduced computer technology in the home office in the late 1960s to track income and costs—such as payroll, food, and supplies—at all its nursing homes. It also recorded the ratio of hours worked in each department in relation to patient-days. But as it expanded quickly and acquired dozens of hospitals, the company hired administrators for each facility to run back-office functions.

In 1974, the firm hired P. Duane "Dewey" Walker to be senior vice president of management systems. He had spent sixteen years at IBM as the architect of its management information system. "I had a very successful career at IBM, but when [a recruiter] described the opportunity to work with two energetic young entrepreneurs, I had to meet you," Walker wrote in a letter to David A. Jones. "You and Wendell had just read an article in the *Harvard Business Review* about what was required to transition from an 'Entrepreneurship' into an 'Enterprise.' Over dinner you explained that would be my mission with Humana. I couldn't resist the challenge."

GAME CHANGE ///

Under a strategy known as the "Humana System," the company, now focused on its hospitals, sought to revolutionize hospital organization, patient care, and productivity. Part of this strategy involved treating patients and doctors as customers, and seeking to understand their values so as to develop services that would meet their specific needs. Opposite: Jones and Bill Barnhart (standing), senior vice president of hospitals, completing the acquisition of a new hospital in the early 1970s.

In cooperation with other executives, Walker
initiated a business planning process for Humana that
was similar to IBM's. Walker recruited an IBM executive,
John Laverty, to help him establish a professional
documentation program for policies and procedures,
and a comprehensive education program. Walker
had been a student of Peter Drucker's at New York
University and told Jones that Drucker had taught him
"to understand how to convert technology change into
economic results."

"Dewey Walker had one idea that transformed the
company," said Jones, "and that was that we needed

one back office. At the time we had fifty hospitals with
administrative officers trying to negotiate with Medicare"
and duplicating other tasks. "Dewey convinced us to put
really good executives in charge and use the available
technology to have one back office." Between 1974 and
1982, when Walker left the company, revenue grew from
$134 million to $1.92 billion.

Humana subsequently ran all of its hospitals
as one institution: one business office, computer
system, and set of billing protocols, and one group
of experienced, long-term associates to manage
relationships with third-party payers. "We started out on
the business side of it under the theory that there were
certain things that could be done centrally and more
efficiently, so more hands-on care could be done on the
scene," said Pollard. "That was what led to the simple
standardization of buildings, chart systems, billing, and
all the back-office functions."

Bob Poston joined the company as a junior
systems programmer in 1975 and worked under
Walker. "At the time we were developing one of the
first computer-based information systems that could
be deployed throughout the hospitals," Poston said.
"Humana had some of the larger IBM systems in the
city. Humana had always had a reputation for seeing
the value of technology and implementing it in new and
unique ways. We invested large amounts of money in the
early stages of hospital automation and administrative
systems." By the 1980s, when the cost per patient
admission averaged fifteen- to-eighteen dollars industry-
wide, Humana's standardized systems provided a better
level of guaranteed service for about five or six dollars.
"That's one of the things that kept me here with the
company all this time—Humana has always seen the
value of technology," said Poston, adding, "and they had
the funds to pay for the really neat toys."

The systems also facilitated centralized purchasing. In 1984, for example, Humana saved about $15 million by choosing one high-quality supplier for most medical products and by having only one distributor for high-volume items. In addition to minimizing expenses, Humana could count on consistent quality and timely delivery. The goal was to have every hospital in the system deliver an identical high-quality experience. "We tried to develop the same processes within each hospital and have every one run the same that way—not unlike McDonald's," said longtime associate Bill Baldwin. "That way you could interchange

professionals more easily. You didn't have to start from scratch to learn processes, and each facility shared a core set of values."

HUMANA DOUBLES IN SIZE

In the fall of 1977, Humana, which ranked third in the industry, made a friendly offer to merge with the company that ranked second—American Medicorp of Bala Cynwyd, Pennsylvania. Humana offered to purchase 75 percent of the outstanding shares for ten dollars cash and 0.3 shares of a new issue of Humana-preferred stock in exchange for each share of the larger firm.

CRUCIAL MONITORING ///

With millions of members, Humana receives more than ninety-five thousand inbound calls per day. Ashley Curry, an analyst at Humana's national command center in Louisville, monitors calls in queue to ensure proper routing while pulling data for daily reporting for call centers around the country.

When American Medicorp rebuffed the offer, Humana launched a hostile takeover. Its rival fought back, filing a suit charging antitrust violations, arguing that a takeover would give Humana a dominant position in the industry. American Medicorp also sued Continental Illinois Bank, charging that the bank had solicited its business and then—while in possession of "confidential, proprietary business information" about the firm—turned around to finance a takeover by Humana, according to press reports. (The suits were ultimately dismissed.)

"Medicorp had some excellent hospitals, including the largest investor-owned hospital in the country" in Las Vegas, recalled Teeple. "Nevertheless, the stock market had never recognized the value of Medicorp, and its stock lagged for years. Medicorp was fighting for its life, and we were fighting to acquire the group of fine facilities at a moderate price. The aggressiveness of Humana and the determined opposition of Medicorp produced a huge, fierce fight for the votes of Medicorp stockholders."

At the time, Earl Reed worked in the reimbursement department, reviewing cost reports. "The relations between us and Medicorp had become very hostile, indeed," he recalled. "So much so that the cost reports we requested came to us in bankers boxes, unstapled and pages mixed together as though they had been through a blender." Reed and two colleagues tried to figure out a rapid method to pull everything together but realized there was no quick fix: "That was the great part about Humana, a true willingness to do what it took to get the job done."

Paperwork nearly thwarted Humana's testimony at one of the trials, recalled William Lomicka, former vice president of finance and treasurer. Lomicka and a colleague, Rick Schweinhart, were preparing additional financial information for Carl Pollard. Late in the evening, they ran to a diner to get something to eat before heading back to work. "When we left, we left our sorted papers everywhere—on desks, on the floor, and on the top of cabinets. Unfortunately, while we were gone, the very efficient cleaning crew had 'cleaned house,' gathering up dozens of pages of the papers we had sorted and prepared for the testimony," Lomicka relayed. "We flew frantically around the building hunting down the cleaning crew and learned that the garbage had been bagged and taken to the basement of the building. Because these were our only copies, we had no other choice but to sort through the garbage bags, digging for our precious, one-of-a-kind papers! I am sure that it was an interesting sight to see Rick and me standing on top of a mountain of garbage bags, carefully opening and sifting through each one. We went through about forty bags, but finally found each and every piece of paper—coffee stains and all."

American Medicorp began seeking a "white knight" to purchase the company. Market rumors had it that the white knight was TWA, owner of the Hilton Hotels & Resorts. Frederick Frank was Humana's investment banker at the time. "Since I knew the chairman of TWA, I called him, and his secretary informed me that he couldn't take the call because he was in a board meeting. I said, 'But it's not a regular board meeting date,' and she responded, 'No, Mr. Frank, this is a very special board meeting,'" Frank recalled. "Well, we certainly had a basis for thinking there might be some substance to the rumor. And it did, indeed, turn out to be correct."

Humana raised its bid and TWA withdrew, but Medicorp continued to resist. Teeple remembered a vote of Humana stockholders, required to satisfy a step in the acquisition process. "Medicorp sent two lawyers to the meeting in an attempt to slow or block Humana stockholders' approval," Teeple explained. "Two

representatives were needed so that one could make
a motion and the other could second it. At the point
in the meeting where the motions were in order, one
Medicorp lawyer made a motion aimed at obstructing
the acquisition. There was no second because the other
Medicorp lawyer had left the room to make a phone call.
As the motion was about to die for lack of a second,
Humana's chairman, David A. Jones, who was conducting
the meeting, graciously seconded the motion so it could
be brought to a vote. The motion from Medicorp was
defeated in a landslide, and the transaction took another
step toward completion."

Reed recalled that when the deal finally went
through, Wendell Cherry showed up on his floor in jeans
and a flannel shirt, carrying four bottles of champagne.
"He put them in my arms and simply said I was to go
get everyone together and have some fun!" Deborah
Triplett, who joined Humana in 1972, recalled that Cherry

promised to sing at a party for associates if the deal went
through. "We had a celebration, and he sang 'Danny Boy'
for a roomful of people, which was amazing," she said.

Humana ultimately paid $303 million for American
Medicorp in cash, stock, and debt. The buyout was
characterized by Philadelphia newspapers as "the shark
that swallowed the whale." The deal doubled the size of
Humana's Florida operations and established a significant
presence on the Pacific coast. Between 1977 and 1978,
Humana grew from sixty to ninety-seven hospitals and
from 15,700 to 36,000 associates. Revenues and net
income more than doubled, to $764 million and $22
million, respectively.

Frank described another potential "merger" that
happened about fifteen months after the acquisition was
complete. Humana's stock was very actively traded on
the New York Stock Exchange, apparently on the basis of
takeover rumors.

"When asked, 'Who is making a hostile offer?' I said,
'It is somewhat incredulous, but the rumor is that General
Motors was making an offer since they had a strategy for
getting their health care costs under control," Frank noted.
"Apparently, GM felt that having a national hospital chain
would give them the infrastructure to help accomplish that
goal.' Wendell, in his inimical style, said, 'Fred, what is the
rumor about the stock price?' I said, 'The rumor is that the
offer will be at fifty dollars a share.' The stock was in the
mid-thirties. Wendell said, 'Hell, there's nothing hostile
about that. Just tell them to call us!'"

A dozen years after Humana had leased its first
facility in Alabama, the company owned ninety hospitals
in twenty-three states and two European countries. By
1980, Humana had grown revenues at an annual rate of
32 percent, exceeding all but two companies in *Financial
World* magazine's annual ranking of ten-year performance
by companies with revenues of more than $500 million.

In June 1980, a Wall Street analyst told the *Wall
Street Transcript*: "With Humana, investors are dealing
with what I believe may be the most aggressive and
smartest major company in the U.S. That's a lot to say
about any company, but Humana's success and the
absolutely uncanny accuracy of its corporate strategy
make it a supportable statement."

CENTERS OF EXCELLENCE

In the early 1980s, Humana began identifying hospitals
with unsurpassed specialty care that served broad
geographic areas. These hospitals were designated
Centers of Excellence. "The Center of Excellence is a
total health care delivery system in its specialty," the
annual report noted in 1981. "It includes an outpatient
diagnostic facility with the latest technologies and
methodologies to diagnose a patient's disease or
disorder—capabilities that may not be otherwise available
in the area. It is a hospital with special expertise in the
form of skilled personnel, medical staff, and equipment to
provide a level of treatment that is beyond the capability
of most community hospitals."

In 1981, the Centers of Excellence included Sunrise
Hospital in Las Vegas, for kidney disease, open-heart
surgery, and neurosurgery; Lucerne General Hospital in
Orlando, for spinal cord injury and open-heart surgery;
Sherman Oaks Community Hospital and Doctors Hospital
in Augusta, for burn treatment; Women's Hospital in
Tampa, for obstetrics and gynecology; and Wellington

Hospital in London, for open-heart and ophthalmic surgery, orthopedics, and renal transplants. The Sherman Oaks Burn Center gained widespread international attention when it provided emergency and continuing care for comedian Richard Pryor in 1980. Several years later, gymnast Mary Lou Retton had an arthroscopic procedure at Humana St. Luke's Hospital in Richmond, Virginia, and just six weeks after surgery won an Olympic gold medal.

Humana would eventually operate two dozen Centers of Excellence in the U.S. and Europe, providing a variety of grants to conduct clinical research.

A NEW DIRECTION IN HEALTH CARE

In the early 1980s, Jones and Cherry recognized the need to explore new solutions for health care delivery. Like the nursing home business before it, the hospital sector was becoming overbuilt, and skyrocketing costs produced pressure in both the private and government sector to get patients out of hospitals as quickly as possible. By 1984, health care costs in the U.S. had reached $393 billion, or 11 percent of the gross national product. Private employers struggled to manage the expenses of benefits, resulting in increased co-payments and higher deductibles for their employees.

Public policy shifted as well: in October 1983, the federal government began phasing out retrospective cost-plus reimbursement of each hospital's expenses as the method of paying for services provided to Medicare patients. Instead, all hospitals would receive set amounts determined in advance and based on the diagnosis and service for each patient. In addition, Medicare began a program of screening for medical necessity before allowing admission to hospitals, resulting in fewer admissions. After peaking in 1981, admissions to acute care hospitals began to decline. In the annual report, Jones warned: "The world is turning, the system

is evolving, and those who do tomorrow what they did yesterday are likely to be caught short."

While other companies continued buying and building facilities, Jones and Cherry jumped at the chance to reinvent their business once again. They envisioned a comprehensive, vertically integrated health care company that provided access to physicians and a prepaid health plan as a unified solution to cost concerns. In 1981, Humana began developing freestanding outpatient clinics in conjunction with physicians in private practice under the brand Humana MedFirst. The centers were open every day with convenient evening and weekend hours for walk-in patients. Physicians treated patients on a normal fee-for-service basis, while Humana provided administrative and support services, and office space on a contractual basis.

Two years later Humana launched its own HMO, called Humana Care Plus. Tested in the Louisville market, the plan was designed to help employers and unions control their health premium costs by guaranteeing a cap on cost increases for several years. Under Humana Care Plus, participants would receive the same benefits as their present coverage and would be free to choose their personal physician. If hospital or outpatient services were required, the associates would have significant incentives to choose Humana hospitals. "The basic goal is to increase use of Humana facilities, driving down unit costs and sharing the savings with the group purchasers," the 1983 annual report noted. "As patient volume increases, unit costs decrease, and the savings allow Humana to guarantee favorable premiums."

Humana grew its new ventures with characteristic aggressiveness: by the end of fiscal year 1985, Humana Care Plus membership had grown nearly nine-fold, to more than 359,000 members in fifty markets, up from ten markets the previous year. The company more than

MILESTONE
ANNIVERSARIES ///

For Humana's tenth
anniversary, the company
commissioned a painting by
associate Sue Chapman. It
depicts milestone events,
including the company's
start in nursing homes
(top left), the construction
of Suburban Hospital in
Louisville (middle right),
the skilled medical care
provided in its hospitals
(bottom left), and the
listing of Extendicare
on the New York Stock
Exchange (middle left). The
painting appeared on the
cover of Humana's 1971
annual report. Opposite:
A caricature celebrating
Humana's twenty-fifth
anniversary, capturing Jones
and Cherry. *In Ignoratione
Est Spes* means "In
Ignorance There Is Hope,"
a reference to the two
founders' ability to turn lack
of experience in the industry
into decades of continued
growth and success.

doubled its Humana MedFirst facilities to 148 centers. Overall revenues rose 10 percent to $2.9 billion, and net income jumped 12 percent to $216 million.

Humana would soon expand offerings to a family of flexible insurance products designed to respond to changing customer needs, and embark on an acquisition spree. Among the companies it purchased was International Medical Centers (IMC) in 1987, which marked Humana's official entry into the Medicare program. The purchase would become crucial to Humana's future, as it grew to become one of the largest and most innovative providers of Medicare benefits in the U.S.

GROWING THE HEALTH PLAN BUSINESS

At first glance, hospitals and insurance companies would seem to have conflicting economic goals—the former earn money when the beds are filled, the latter save money when they're empty. But other firms, such as Kaiser Permanente, founded by West Coast industrialist Henry Kaiser, had successfully managed both hospitals and insurance. "We really saw it as a way that health care should be delivered," said Pollard.

Jones said the idea to move into HMOs came from an experience with a Humana hospital in Phoenix. "We had a successful hospital that had a contract with a large HMO, and in one year the contract was lost to a competitor hospital. We lost a tremendous amount of business in that hospital," he recalled. "A hospital is like an airline; it's a fixed cost business. If the plane takes off empty you still have to pay all the costs. So we took a big bath in that year, and that's when I decided we needed to protect ourselves and look at the HMO business ourselves as a defensive measure."

The concept was simple: insurance members would use Humana hospitals. Humana would share the revenue from higher occupancy with the purchasers of insurance by offering lower premiums. Premiums would be guaranteed to rise no faster than the cost-of-living index for the life of the contract—up to four years. Humana would still have to negotiate rates with doctors and specialists (while under the Kaiser model, those professionals worked directly for the firm).

At first the model worked quite well, and by 1985, Humana Care Plus expanded to all metropolitan areas that contained Humana hospitals. In 1986, Humana introduced the insurance into markets where it owned MedFirst offices, and membership grew 32 percent, to 616,500 members. Humana also expanded into new business lines, testing a Medicare supplemental policy to fill the gaps left by the government program, as well as a comprehensive risk plan to provide all Medicare benefits at a fixed fee paid by the government.

But then challenges began to emerge. When the insurance industry tried to manage skyrocketing health care costs for their clients, physicians who did not like the negotiated rates or terms—such as pre-admission approval requirements—retaliated by sending their patients to hospitals other than Humana's. The payments to those hospitals were far higher than the costs would have been at a Humana facility. Overall costs began to surpass Humana's guaranteed premiums. Meanwhile,

rival insurers, who couldn't compete with Humana's low insurance rates because they did not control hospitals, also steered their members elsewhere. The hospital business began to suffer as a result.

Humana chief operating officer Jim Murray said the concept was ahead of its time. "Mr. Jones was pretty visionary in terms of his understanding that the real way to control medical spending is to create a Kaiser-like model," said Murray. "Aligning the players in the delivery of care and focusing on the quality of outcomes is the holy grail, and unfortunately we were not able to pull that off at that time."

At the same time, results at the MedFirst Division began to disappoint. In 1986, Humana decided to reduce the number from 153 units to about one hundred, and a year later sold the entire division. In 1986, after a quarter century in business and fourteen consecutive years of improved earnings, Humana's net income declined 75 percent to $54.5 million.

After several years of hard lessons and extensive adjustments, the group health division significantly improved its book of business and introduced a new line of flexible multiple-options contracts. It also signed eight thousand physicians' contracts. The division concentrated its efforts in sixteen markets where Humana had its strongest hospital presence and strengthened ties to the hospital division through the introduction of a specialized treatment facility benefit. The feature offered access to the high quality care available at Humana's twenty-four Centers of Excellence.

NETWORKING OPPORTUNITIES ///

Within the Humana organization, care is taken to ensure that all market office networks remain up and running. Casandra Montgomery (left) and Michele Miller, who work in network operations for the Chicago market office, speak with Roddrick T. Davis, DSI.

Under the terms of the benefit, a member requiring highly specialized treatment that was covered by the plan and available at one of the centers was covered for transportation and treatment costs. One family member would also be covered for transportation and lodging costs.

Humana changed its contracts and underwriting, and in 1988, net income rebounded 24 percent to $227 million on revenues of $3.4 billion, a 16 percent rise. The group health division accounted for nearly 11 percent of the total patient days in Humana hospitals—up from about 7 percent the previous year. Several new acquisitions helped boost membership in the group, which reached 791,000 members, up from 555,000 the previous year, improving economies of scale.

A DEVASTATING LOSS AND A DIVISION

In 1989, revenues surpassed $4 billion; in just six years, the health plans had grown into a $1 billion business with more than one million members. Net income rose to $255 million. The company employed more than 55,000 people and was chosen as one of "Twenty Corporations Best Prepared for the 1990s" by *Forbes* magazine. Humana would open the new decade with several key acquisitions—the 240,000-member Michael Reese Health Plan and its affiliated 652-bed hospital in Chicago; an 80,000-member health maintenance organization in Kansas City; and Community Health in Cincinnati, which had 13,000 members.

Quality remained the core pursuit at Humana's hospitals. In the first half of 1991, the Joint Commission on Accreditation of Healthcare Organizations surveyed 581 non-Humana hospitals, and just 4 percent received the organization's highest designation, the Accreditation with Commendation. Of the twenty-five Humana hospitals surveyed in the same period, seventeen achieved the highest designation.

But ultimately, Humana was unable to reconcile the conflict between its hospitals and insurance plans, and formulated a plan to split the divisions into two separate companies. Then in February 1990, Wendell Cherry was diagnosed with a brain tumor. He died seventeen months later at age fifty-five. "It was heartbreaking then and still is," said Jones. "I was with him every day in the last days of his illness, and he told me I was the best friend he ever had. Hardly a day goes by that I don't think about Wendell and how he might react to this or that."

In 1992, Humana made a formal announcement that it would separate the hospital and health plan businesses into two separate companies. "It was probably the most difficult time of my life for a number of reasons," said Carl Pollard, who ran the hospitals. "You were negotiating things that would have an impact on both companies for any number of years. It was not a pleasant experience, but we got through it. I stayed with the hospitals and left Humana at the time of the split. The hospital business was a good business—I thought it was a better business than David did. He was convinced that insurance was the wave of the future and made a tremendous success out of the insurance products."

On February 18, 1993, Humana shareholders overwhelmingly approved a plan to separate the hospital operations from its health insurance business, with ninety-six million of 159 million voting shares in favor of the split. The seventy-seven Humana hospitals were renamed Galen Health Care, Inc. The health plan side, which insured 1.7 million people, retained the Humana name, and on a revenue basis was the largest publicly traded managed care firm. Under the terms of the deal, shareholders received one share in Galen for each share of Humana stock owned. Galen Health Care was a $4 billion company with $460 million in pretax earnings; Humana was a $2.8 billion health insurance company with $6 million in pretax earnings. The two companies began trading separately on the New York Stock Exchange.

"I stayed with the insurance side because I thought it was more interesting," said Jones. "I didn't like leaving the hospital business. I loved that business." Shortly after the split, Galen Health Care merged with a competitor, Columbia, while Humana continued to build its business through the 1990s with key acquisitions: Physician Corporation of America (PCA), ChoiceCare, and Employers Health Insurance Company. In 1997, David A. Jones would retire as chief executive after thirty-six years of leading the company but retain the title of chairman.

David A. Jones, Jr., said that although his father had built Humana into a leading hospital firm, he was ready to move on. "I don't think my dad and Mr. Cherry ever looked back. They didn't when they exited the nursing home business and the mobile home business. They were strong believers that leaving behind yesterday's success is one of the most important components of building tomorrow's. They also took great pride in the achievements of individuals who came up through Humana and went on to other things."

A STRUGGLE AND A NEW DIRECTION

Between 1993 and 1998, Humana grew rapidly and achieved some major milestones. In 1995, for example, the company won the first of several major contracts from the U.S. Department of Defense to offer health benefits to millions of military families and veterans, a program called TRICARE. But in its other divisions, Humana began to struggle with pricing issues as the cost of care rose faster than the premiums the company charged its members.

Former board chairman and current board member Jones, Jr., said the problems were industry-wide, and the underlying cause complex. "Back then there was an incredible debate among Wall Street analysts and people in the company about whether there is a cycle in managed care: when profits are high, new entrants come into the market and drive down the price of coverage; everyone loses money, and then companies exit the business," Jones explained. "In the 1990s, it was unclear to both Wall Street and within Humana how much control over costs the company really had. We had two or

I don't think my dad and Mr. Cherry ever looked back. They didn't when they exited the nursing home business and the mobile home business. They were strong believers that leaving behind yesterday's success is one of most important components of building tomorrow's.

—DAVID A. JONES, JR.
FORMER CHAIRMAN OF THE BOARD AND CURRENT BOARD MEMBER

three earnings surprises where we completely missed our own forecasts and performed really badly."

Humana Chief Operating Officer Jim Murray said the timing was also problematic: the industry would set pricing in the fall, collect premiums, and set aside reserves to cover costs when medical bills arrived the following year. "We didn't have good visibility on costs and weren't putting them in our premiums quickly enough and adequately enough," he said. "Back then a lot of the businesses that we wrote insurance for renewed their coverage in January, and we were putting prices on the street in the third and fourth quarter of a particular year without the information systems in place to properly charge or set premium levels for the following January.

"What was generally happening is we would have really bad news around March and April every year," Murray continued, "because we would start to count claims with the new effective period, and lo and behold, premiums from the third and fourth quarter weren't adequate. Also, companies were shadow-pricing each other to gain market share, so underwriting controls in the industry were not what they should have been." As one health care analyst told the New York Times in 1998, "The industry is offering $1,000 in benefits, when they can only afford to provide $750."

Humana reorganized its leadership, and business went smoothly for a while, "and then—boom!—another big earnings blow up," Jones Jr. recalled. "The business had lost its way. I don't mean in a financial sense, because we never lost confidence that we could figure out how to make money. It was a big enough business, and it was clear you could turn it around and make it go. But it was becoming a commodity insurance business. The mission wasn't exciting."

Humana's difficulties prompted merger talks with Minneapolis-based United Healthcare, which in May 1998 offered to buy the company in a stock swap valued at $5.5 billion. The combined firm would have been the nation's largest HMO, with 10 million members. Moreover, a merged company would enjoy a significant advantage in controlling costs. When the acquisition was announced, United Healthcare chairman Dr. William McGuire predicted eventual savings of $100 million to $250 million, primarily by eliminating administrative costs and lowering payments to hospitals. "We got an attractive offer from a seemingly solid company, and it appeared to be the best thing for the shareholders," said Jones Jr.

But in late summer 1998, United Healthcare reported an unexpected $900 million charge in its

**A REUNION OF
THE DIRECTORS ///**

All current and former
directors gathered for the
retirement of David A. Jones
and Michael E. Gellert in
2005. The directors included
(from left to right) Carl
Pollard, John R. Hall, Frank
A. D'Amelio, Kurt J. Hilzinger,
David A. Jones, Jr., Gellert,
John W. Landrum, William C.
Ballard, Jr., Mike McCallister,
Jones, W. Roy Dunbar, Dr. W.
Ann Reynolds, Lewis "Sonny"
Bass, J. David Grissom, Hilary
Boone, Jr., and Irwin Lerner.

fiscal second quarter, causing its stock to plunge 28 percent. It lost $2.9 billion in market value in a single day. After the sell-off, Humana's shareholders would have received only $3.1 billion from the acquisition, far less than the $5.5 billion the company had agreed upon. "We disengaged because United Healthcare identified some problems with its operations," a Humana spokesman told the *New York Times* in August 1998. "That made it clear that Humana would be more successful on our own." In addition, the companies had vastly different views on the Medicare market: while a portion of United Healthcare's $900 million charge was to scale back its Medicare

offerings, Humana ranked as one of the industry's most prosperous providers.

"Once United blew up it was unthinkable to do the deal," said Jones Jr. "They had a material adverse change in their circumstance, and the deal we had signed up for wasn't there anymore. It didn't make any sense to do the deal, especially since their problems seemed to surprise them. The problem with the business in those days was we were not able to forecast or control costs. All of a sudden we realized, 'They have the same problem, and if we all have the same problem, we might as well just solve it ourselves.'"

HEART-TO-HEART ///

In addition to in-person guidance related to their health care coverage, Humana's Guidance Centers offer activities to promote social well-being. Isabel Micocci, MarketPoint sales representative (standing), speaks with members (left to right) Anita Cawein, Mareta Stay, and Lynn Fass at a Valentine's Day party at the Tamarac, Florida, Guidance Center.

A REVITALIZED MISSION

In 1999, David A. Jones returned to Humana as interim chief executive officer and created an office of the chairman, consisting of himself, three senior executives—Mike McCallister, Jim Murray, and Ken Fasola—and two health care consultants from the firm SSB Solutions, Dr. Jacque Sokolov and Steve Bennett. The assignments were to resolve the performance issues, lay out the company's strategic direction, and examine ways that emerging technologies could change the business.

At a board meeting in November 1999, the company leaders presented a vision of next-generation health plans, tentatively known as digital health plans, to the board of directors. "The digital health plan was fundamentally different from any health plan that had

come before, largely because it allowed real-time consumer interaction with the plan itself in multiple areas and with multiple touch points," Sokolov explained in a letter to Jones. "The plan would provide access through at least four portals: the health plan's coverage and eligibility administration; medical information; consumer connectivity; and provider connectivity. The foundation for a combination of real-time connectivity and consumer-facing technology was outlined." It would require a massive $500 million investment at a time when the company's market capitalization was under $1 billion and its stock was closing at less than five dollars a share.

A three-hour debate ensued, and the board split into two camps: those who felt the digital health plan represented an enormous risk that would overtax Humana's weakened resources, and those who thought the company's future depended on its implementation. Jones, after patiently listening and contributing throughout the protracted discussion, finally had enough, Sokolov recalled: "He smacked his hand on the table—in a moment reminiscent of Soviet Premier Nikita Khrushchev at the United Nations—and said, 'I have heard many learned opinions this evening from many learned individuals and directors. The directors represent academic institutions, medical insight, and management creativity. But one voice we have not heard tonight is the shareholder's. What would the shareholders say about this decision that could seal the fate of this corporation? As the single largest shareholder, I will tell you what the shareholders would say. They would say let's do it.'"

Humana established an independent company called Emphesys, located adjacent to its headquarters, to hedge the $500 million bet that Humana could deliver and launch the first digital health plan twenty-two months later. Humana executive vice president Gene Shields took the helm of the new firm. The gamble was enormous, but launching Emphesys "was not as risky as *not* doing it," said Jones. "The economy is strewn with companies left behind by the digital revolution. There isn't any business or enterprise in the world right now that doesn't need to understand how changing technology will impact its business."

The lead-up to the launch of the Emphesys digital health plan "was a lot like planning for the Normandy invasion," Sokolov noted. "Technical issues had to be overcome, and key benefit design issues had to be decided upon. Connectivity issues had to be finalized, and internal Humana constituencies had to be managed. But the Humana team in place was up to the task."

McCallister saw Emphesys as the catalyst for the next generation of managed care. "Individual consumers are going to have a lot more financial involvement in the cost of things as they move through health care," McCallister told *Business First*, a Louisville business publication, in 2001. "We're building capabilities both from a product perspective and from a technology perspective to meet that employer-financed, consumer-centric health benefits product, which we think is the next thing after managed care as we know it today."

"That bold decision at the [1999] board meeting paid off," Sokolov wrote in a letter to Jones. "Humana has become a very different company than it otherwise would have been, and a team of remarkable people at many levels executed a concept that a lot of really smart people didn't think could be done."

From 2001 to 2006, Humana grew from six million to eleven million beneficiaries and from a market cap of less than $1 billion to $10 billion. The stock price also rose from five dollars to sixty dollars a share. Key acquisitions in this era included the Ochsner Health Plan of Louisiana, CarePlus Health Plans of Florida, and CHA Health. Confident in its new direction, Humana would be uniquely positioned to apply the lessons of consumer-driven health care to private plans for Medicare, which was on the verge of major reform.

THE GROWTH OF THE MEDICARE BUSINESS

As a leading hospital company in the 1980s, Humana began dedicating itself to learning how to best serve senior consumers—the fastest growing segment of the population and a demographic that uses hospitals five times as often as its younger counterparts. In 1987, Humana launched a "Humana Seniors Association," a national organization with its own board of directors, to offer seniors reliable health care information, social get-togethers, and community involvement.

**A FORCE FOR
FREEWHEELIN AND
WELL-BEING ///**

Throughout its fifty years
in the health care industry,
Humana has engaged the
public with programs that
offer avenues to health
and well-being. Trisha
Finnegan, a consultant for
the consumer innovation
team who served as a
core team member for
the Freewheelin bike-
sharing programs at
the 2008 Democratic
and Republican national
conventions as well as
the 2009 National Senior
Games, reviews her notes.

For a twelve dollar annual fee, members were given access to a full-time registered nurse advisor to help them take total advantage of community resources; discounts for travel, wellness programs, and other services; and an insurance specialist to assist in filing their insurance and Medicare forms, relieving them of piles of daunting paperwork. In just twelve months, 121,000 members had joined. The emphasis on seniors laid the groundwork for the company's later focus on Medicare plans.

In 1987, Humana grew its Medicare business with the purchase of International Medical Centers (IMC), the largest HMO in Florida. IMC had 130,000 members, 85 percent covered by the Medicare contract program. Known as Medicare Advantage Plans, these HMOs offer comprehensive benefits to enrollees, with typically low or no premiums, as well as low deductibles and co-payments for members who choose doctors and hospitals within the plan's network. By contrast, seniors who choose the traditional Medicare program can see any physician who accepts Medicare, but they pay significant monthly premiums (an average of $96 in 2008). In addition, those seniors must cover 20

percent of the cost of doctor visits, outpatient services, lab work, and diagnostics tests such as X-rays. As member John Nelson wrote to Humana: "Our doctor bills and subscription costs have gone down drastically. Every time we went to see the doctor, it was about fifty dollars; now it is fifteen dollars. I am on five different daily pills, and my wife is on three. The cost has dropped from about $160 per month to about thirty-two dollars per month."

As one of the first participants in the Medicare HMO program, Humana had long believed there would be new private sector opportunities for those who stayed the course. That opportunity arose six years later, when the federal government approved the Medicare Modernization Act (MMA) of 2003, the largest overhaul in the thirty-eight-year history of the program. The new law, which would take effect January 1, 2006, strengthened the traditional Medicare HMO product by offering subsidies to participating insurers, and introduced a variety of prospects for other areas of participation by the private sector. For example, PPOs were the most popular form of health insurance in the U.S. at the time, but prior to the legislation, they were not widely available to seniors. Humana launched a senior PPO product that was positioned between HMOs and traditional Medigap policies that offer supplemental health insurance.

But the most significant change was the introduction of the Medicare Prescription Drug Plan (PDP), an entitlement benefit for prescription drugs that also went into effect January 1, 2006. "The passage of the MMA in 2003 started the resurgence of Medicare as a strong business opportunity for those companies that understand, based on varied and successful experience, how to work with the government and senior citizens," the 2003 annual report stated. "This has re-established Medicare as a business line that is likely to bring us accelerating growth.

LITTLE HOMES AWAY
FROM HOME ///
Humana understands that
health and well-being go far
beyond doctors visits and
prescription medication.
Health and Wellness Centers
known by Medicare members
as "Las Casitas" are attached
to CAC-Florida Medical
Center clinics and provide
opportunities for exercise
and socializing. Left: Arnold
Smelson and Nancy La Rocca
at the Guidance Center in
Tamarac, Florida. Opposite:
Maria T. Romero (standing)
chats with Orlinda Barreiro
(center) and Blanca Acosta
as they play bingo at the Bird
Road CAC.

By serving the Medicare HMO market longer and more successfully than almost all of our competitors, we learned 'early lessons' in health care consumerism."

Medicare Part D, the prescription drug benefit, "made specific participation requirements around consumer-facing technologies and many of the very same interaction-focused capabilities we made part of the original digital health plan concept," Sokolov stated. "The company's farsightedness and willingness to bet on the future and invest in those capabilities was

instrumental in its success in the Medicare Advantage and Medicare Part D space."

Private insurers couldn't begin selling their Medicare plans until November 15, 2005. But Humana had learned over time that seniors prefer face-to-face interactions where they can be educated one-on-one. So the company unveiled its "Let's Talk" program in the summer of 2005, in which mobile recreational vehicles visited more than three hundred cities to educate people about the new program and raise national awareness of

the Humana brand prior to the selling period. In addition, Humana knew seniors wanted the ability to enroll in the new Medicare options through a variety of formats. To offer convenience, Humana struck a national alliance with Walmart, in which Humana sales representatives sold Medicare products in 3,200 Walmart, Sam's Club, and Neighborhood Market stores across the U.S. About 60 percent of the company's 2005 enrollments came through those locations. Humana also partnered with 17,000 State Farm insurance agents, who served as effective sales distribution channels throughout the enrollment period. In addition, Humana developed the capacity for e-signatures and launched a robust web site to facilitate one-on-one enrollment. As it turned out, 39 percent of the first-year PDP enrollees signed up online.

The year 2006 was a transformative one for Humana. The company grew from $14 billion in annual revenue to $21 billion. By December 31, 2006, Humana had added nearly four million Medicare members. With members in all fifty states, Humana became one of the top two competitors in the new PDP area, vastly exceeding its membership expectations. Humana ranked first in Florida and second in Texas in a J. D. Power and Associates survey of customer satisfaction among PDP members.

Value-added service would be critical to retaining the new Medicare members, Humana decided. The company rolled out comprehensive care coordination services such as case management, social service coordination, home and hospital visits, cognitive assessments, and caregiver training. It also launched a "Personal Nurse" program in which highly skilled registered nurses provided support, information, and resources to members with acute or chronic health conditions. And the Humana "Active Outlook" program provided a comprehensive menu of health, wellness,

and healthy lifestyle offerings, including PositScience—a computer-based brain fitness program promoting mental acuity—and the SilverSneakers program. In 2010, one in five of Humana's 1.8 million eligible members participated in SilverSneakers.

In addition, in 2009 Humana began opening Guidance Centers in cities where it has large concentrations of members, staffed by local Humana sales and service personnel. Anyone can visit to access information and receive service related to Humana health plans, whether it's questions about health insurance claims, proof of enrollment, payments, and correspondences with Humana, or help finding health care providers. The centers also serve as a meeting place for all community members, offering expert lectures; wellness seminars; healthy cooking demonstrations; social activities and special events, such as craft courses; and video games that promote physical activity. By 2011, Humana had sixteen centers in five Midwestern states, plus Florida, Texas, Arizona, and Nevada.

Dorothy Miller, a Missouri retiree who lives on $746 a month, wrote to Humana about her experience with the company's Gold Choice Plan: "After I joined I soon received an invitation in the mail to see the film *Casablanca*. I was somewhat surprised. Not only did they send me the ticket to see the movie, they supplied the snacks." Not long after, she learned about the SilverSneakers program at her local YMCA. "I really looked forward to this because I have been sick for four years and was just about past going. Since I joined SilverSneakers my energy level has improved at least 85 to 90 percent. I look forward to my Tuesday and Thursday mornings. Now that I am feeling much better, I plan on using the equipment at the YMCA to help me lose weight and feel 100 percent. I love all the literature you send for me to read about improving my health."

ENERGY TO SPARE ///

Humana Guidance Centers offer fun activities that help members stay healthy and agile through their SilverSneakers fitness program. In addition to exercise classes, the Guidance Centers provide options like a Wii Bowling League for members.

04

—

DISTINGUISHED BY INNOVATION

INNOVATION EPICENTER ///

Located within Humana's Louisville headquarters is the Innovation Center, a sweeping space devoted to understanding Humana's customers and developing new ways to improve their health and well-being through learning, health-related games, and exploration. Katie Sexton (facing), a consultant for consumer innovation, meets with process manager Karen Moss in the Innovation Center's Immersion Room to discuss the coordination and facilitation of the center's displays and prototypes.

INNOVATION IS ABOUT CREATING NEW CONCEPTS, PRODUCTS, AND SERVICES THAT SATISFY TODAY'S NEEDS—AND COMING UP WITH USEFUL TECHNOLOGIES THAT PEOPLE HAVEN'T IMAGINED YET. WHO HAD THE NEED FOR AN IPOD UNTIL AN IPOD CAME ALONG?

—RAJA RAJAMANNAR
CHIEF INNOVATION AND MARKETING OFFICER

CUTTING-EDGE PROJECT MANAGEMENT ///
Tonya Walsh, a project manager in the applications engineering group, aids her team with the development and implementation of production features by employing up-to-the-minute project management strategies.

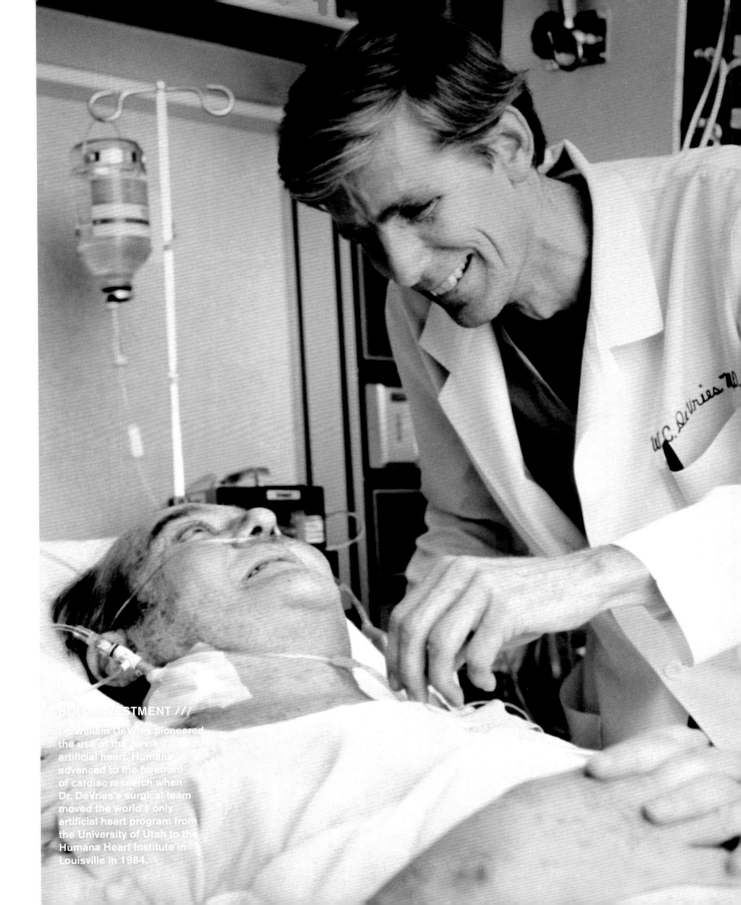

BOLD INVESTMENT ///

Dr. William DeVries pioneered the use of the Jarvik-7 artificial heart. Humana advanced to the forefront of cardiac research when Dr. DeVries's surgical team moved the world's only artificial heart program from the University of Utah to the Humana Heart Institute in Louisville in 1984.

In the mid-1970s, Humana introduced a novel idea to its hospitals: the sixty-second emergency room response. "When we started out it was simple: if you go to our emergency room, you'll be seen by someone with medical training in one minute," explained former Humana executive Carl Pollard. "We established a triage system so a medical professional was there to evaluate every person who came in the door and see the sickest person as fast as possible. The industry's standard greeting was, 'How will you pay?' Humana's was, 'Why are you here, and what medicines are you taking?'"

Putting the practice into operation required a physical reorganization of emergency room departments so a nurse would be the first person a patient would see. A triage nurse would obtain medically necessary information, try to make the patient comfortable, and assign priorities for seeing available physicians. "The fact that such an obvious change is revolutionary in the hospital industry indicates how little attention has been paid by hospitals to the values of patients," the 1975 annual report noted. The company "is convinced that understanding its customers and their values is vital." Competitors soon followed suit.

"We did market research and discovered what people wanted in a hospital more than anything else was a dependable emergency room," said Humana cofounder David A. Jones. "We had all been in the emergency room with kids with sports fractures, and in most hospitals the first person you see is a clerk who wants to get your insurance information. We

Humana's history has been distinguished by innovation—from the 1960s, with its progressive nursing homes; to the 1970s, when Humana brought new thinking to site plans and hospital construction, medical technology, productivity, and standards for quality of care; to the company's Centers of Excellence program of the 1980s, which produced medical advances such as groundbreaking artificial heart research and historic transplants. Over the past two decades, Humana has introduced another array of innovations that put the consumer at the center of health care decision-making. They include technology to provide actionable information in real time; analytical data tools to identify and prevent potential disease and chronic conditions in members years before they develop; technology-driven wellness and incentive programs; and coordinated, personalized care to help members manage complex health conditions. Moreover, Humana has focused on using technology to improve efficiency and productivity of the administrative side of the business so physicians and other service providers can focus their time and energy on their patients' well-being.

INNOVATIONS IN HOSPITAL DESIGN AND SERVICE

Extendicare brought immediate innovations to its newly constructed facilities. The firm took a "campus" approach to hospital design, providing space for doctors' offices and clinics, and ancillary facilities such as radiology, laboratory, pharmacy, electrocardiograph, and physical therapy, among others. "The proximity of a doctor's office to the hospital can mean a significant saving in time for him," the 1971 annual report noted. "Additionally, it permits the doctor to use the hospital's equipment for his outpatients, avoiding the duplication of expensive X-ray and testing equipment." In 1975, the company built

borrowed from the military the idea of a triage nurse and physically changed the nursing station so that when you came in, a nurse was the first person you saw. Fifty percent of hospital admissions come through emergency rooms, so as our emergency service expanded, it propelled our inpatient census, market share, and profitability while fulfilling consumers' most basic hospital needs."

That philosophy has been core to Humana's success: transform insights and ideas into new processes and technologies that add value to the customer experience; make it easier for medical professionals to focus on patients; and drive practical results for shareholders.

one of the first outpatient surgery facilities in the U.S. at Suburban Hospital in Louisville.

Extendicare's facilities also offered state-of-the-art technology. Early on it hired several physicians whose sole job was to identify and research promising new technologies and devices, said Pollard. "For example, we had the first lithotripter—a non-invasive device that pulverizes kidney stones using shock waves. They're very common now, but they weren't thirty years ago." At the 1973 dedication ceremonies for a hospital in Winnfield, Louisiana, Senator Russell Long noted that the facilities were "on a par with the best that exist in the country"—including Bethesda Naval Hospital in Maryland. "I was impressed to notice that the equipment you have in this hospital is the same equipment that is available to treat the president of the United States," Long said.

In addition, Extendicare established its hospitals as centers of learning for medical and nursing students. In 1970, St. Joseph's Hospital in Louisville had twenty-two residents and eleven interns continuing their medical educations at the facility, and 116 students enrolled in the School of Nursing. Extendicare also reached out to the wider community, offering instruction in emergency medical care, CPR, natural childbirth, teenage babysitting, smoking cessation, stress-reduction, and nutrition.

THE ARTIFICIAL HEART IMPLANT

In 1984, Humana made a bold investment in cardiac research that would turn the brand into a household name. The journey began three decades earlier with a Michigan surgeon named Forest Dewey Dodrill, who made history by using a mechanical heart mechanism to keep a patient alive while he performed an operation to repair a damaged valve. For physician-inventors, the holy grail was a device that could actually replace the human

heart, since thousands of patients were dying every year waiting for organs to become available for transplant.

In 1982, a surgical team headed by Dr. William DeVries at the University of Utah implanted the first artificial heart intended for permanent use in a Seattle dentist, Barney Clark. American physician Robert Jarvik invented the device, the Jarvik-7, a pump made of plastic and titanium and powered by compressed air. The air was delivered by an external compressor through tubes that passed into Clark's body through incisions in his abdomen. The Jarvik-7 kept Clark alive for 112 days before he succumbed to complications caused by the implant.

DeVries, the only surgeon authorized to implant artificial hearts at the time, had received permission from the Food and Drug Administration to do seven implants but had become frustrated by the bureaucracy in Utah. The university required a case-by-case review, and funding for the program depended mainly on private benefactors. Dr. Allan Lansing, a noted Louisville heart surgeon who had established the Humana Heart Institute International at Humana Hospital Audubon, acquainted Jones with DeVries's dilemma. Lansing had worked with DeVries on animal artificial heart implants. After meeting with Lansing, Jones offered to fund up to one hundred artificial heart implants as long as medical progress continued to be made.

In July 1984, DeVries relocated his heart program to Louisville. "The opportunities are better for less red tape" at Humana, he told the *New York Times*. Inventor Jarvik commented, "Humana's support strengthens the artificial heart program immeasurably and will hasten the day when it will become available to the estimated 50,000 patients per year whose lives could be saved."

Bruce Perkins, the administrator of Humana Hospital Audubon in the 1980s, said it was a heady time for the company. "It was really exciting; it was cutting

PIONEERING MEDICINE ///

In 1984, the Humana Heart Institute in Louisville became the new center for the artificial heart program and the groundbreaking research of Dr. William DeVries and his surgical team. DeVries implanted the first artificial heart for permanent use in 1982, but was in need of further funding. After David A. Jones learned about DeVries's dilemma from Dr. Allan Lansing, Humana pledged to fund up to one hundred implants, as long as medical progress continued to be made. DeVries performed the world's second artificial heart transplant, in Louisville in 1984. Right: A signed photograph of Dr. William DeVries and his patient, fifty-two-year-old William Schroeder, the recipient of the second artificial heart. Opposite: The May 1985 edition of *Life* magazine, featuring Dr. DeVries and Schroeder on the cover.

edge—we had press coverage across the world," said Perkins, now senior vice president, health care delivery systems and clinical processes. "Bill DeVries was a very charismatic fellow and had a passion for what he was doing." Perkins said the hospital went through multiple trial runs before the first surgery. "We practiced and practiced at the hospital so we wouldn't make a mistake. We had a redundancy of equipment and personnel so that when we went into the operating room for the procedure there was a second team on standby—because literally the eyes of the world were on us." Nearly one thousand journalists representing four hundred worldwide media outlets descended on Louisville in November 1984 to cover the

second heart implant by DeVries. Humana rented the Kentucky International Convention Center to accommodate the media, setting up a press conference room, editing area, and individual work stations for reporters, who came from as far away as Australia. Meanwhile, detectives from the Louisville police were stationed in the parking lot after Humana received a bomb threat from someone upset by the prospect of a "bionic" heart. "We got a lot of mail to the effect of 'if you cut out a human heart, you're cutting out a soul,'" said Perkins.

On November 25, 1984, fifty-two-year-old William Schroeder became the second human recipient of the Jarvik-7. The Jasper, Indiana, retired federal worker was a father of six and a longtime smoker. He had a heart attack in 1983 and subsequent coronary bypass surgery, but it failed to stabilize his deteriorating heart. He sought out the artificial heart team through his hometown physician.

Schroeder's operation was initially a success. When he awoke from sedation, DeVries asked Schroeder if they could get anything for him, and Schroeder replied: "I'd like a cold Coors." (The media covered his response, and the next day a Coors truck showed up in the hospital parking lot.) Schroeder also received a phone call from President Ronald Reagan after the surgery. "The president asked, 'Is there anything we can do for you?' and Schroeder complained that he was having trouble getting his disability checks," Perkins said. A representative from the Treasury Department flew to Louisville the next day to deliver a check.

During an outing in the hospital parking lot after the surgery, Schroeder told reporters he was feeling "real fine." It appeared Schroeder might be able to attend his son's wedding, scheduled for the next month, for which he'd already been fitted for a tuxedo. Schroeder and his wife moved to a nearby apartment, making Schroeder

> We practiced and practiced at the hospital so we wouldn't make a mistake. We had a redundancy of equipment and personnel so that when we went into the operating room for the procedure, there was a second team on standby—because literally the eyes of the world were on us.

—BRUCE PERKINS

SENIOR VICE PRESIDENT, HEALTH CARE DELIVERY SYSTEMS AND CLINICAL PROCESSES

the first artificial heart patient to live outside a hospital. In an interview with the *New York Times* about two weeks after his implant surgery, Schroeder said he felt "super," inviting the reporter to put a hand on his chest and feel the mechanical device inside beating away like "an old-time threshing machine."

But eighteen days after the implant, Schroeder suffered a stroke, the beginning of multiple debilitating complications. "The stroke was difficult for the staff and Bill DeVries and Schroeder's family," said Perkins. "Schroeder lived for a long time after his stroke, not fully cognizant of what was going on. But his oldest son was scheduled to be married and wanted his dad there for the wedding. The surgeons thought it was unsafe for him to leave the hospital. So we dressed up the lobby like a chapel and sent buses up to Indiana and brought the wedding party and the priest. Rob Jarvik came in for the wedding and brought his wife. We had the wedding right in the lobby of the hospital." Schroeder died 620 days after the implant. At his funeral, DeVries said that Schroeder was a man "who pushed the seeds of a tree into the ground knowing he may never live in its shade."

In February 1985, three months after Schroeder received his artificial heart, Murray Haydon, a fifty-eight-year-old assembly-line worker at the Louisville Ford plant,

became the third implant recipient. Haydon suffered from severe congestive heart failure caused by cardiomyopathy, a deterioration of the heart muscle, and by the time he was accepted to the heart program, he had only a few weeks to live. His family had read about Schroeder's surgery and asked their family doctor to approach Humana. After his implant, Haydon suffered just one mild stroke, because the team applied the lessons from Schroeder's case and put Haydon on a drug therapy to prevent blood clots. Haydon was eventually moved to a private room next to Schroeder's, and on the first day they visited and shook hands. Haydon said, "We'll have to get together now that we're next-door neighbors." Haydon went more than a year before suffering another stroke, although he never left the hospital. He died in June 1986, 488 days after his surgery.

Donna Hazle Glanzman was the hospital's director of marketing and public relations at the time. "Though we were all proud of and confident in the work being done, we had accepted the reality that this truly was an experiment and that there may be unexpected setbacks," she wrote in a letter to Jones.

Within two years of Haydon's surgery, physician teams worldwide had implanted forty-nine Jarvik-7 hearts, primarily as temporary bridges to transplantation. DeVries was close to performing his fifth artificial-heart transplant in January 1988 when a human donor heart was found for the patient. Two years later the FDA withdrew its approval of the Jarvik-7, ending the innovative program. "Although Schroeder had a stroke, he wouldn't have traded the year-plus that he got, and Murray's family was remarkably pleased they had him around for a while," said Perkins. "We certainly had our detractors and supporters through it all. It was a big learning experience and an incredible commitment on the part of Humana. David A. Jones and Wendell Cherry had such great vision; they saw things others didn't see and had the courage to go after them."

Humana would continue to invest in cardiac medical research long after it exited the hospital business in 1993. In 2006, for example, Humana partnered in a four-year, $30 million international initiative to develop an inexpensive method to identify "vulnerable plaque," a leading cause of heart attacks. There are no tests to detect the plaque, so people don't realize they should seek treatment that could help. NBC journalist Tim Russert, for example, died of a massive heart attack just two months after performing well on a stress test. Humana recruited 7,300 health-plan members in three areas of the country to volunteer for what was the largest biomarkers study of its kind, taking imaging and lab equipment out in trucks to volunteers' homes to ensure the study would have a wider, more diverse sample of participants.

THE HUMANA INNOVATION CENTER

Reaching out to consumers in a cardiac study is just one example of the initiatives that developed out of Humana's long-standing commitment to innovation. When Mike McCallister became chief executive officer in 2000, he initiated a shift from the old world of managed care toward a new vision of consumer-centric health care. To help guide Humana through the change, the company launched a formal Innovation Center on the tenth floor of its Louisville headquarters. Visitors are welcome at the center, which features interactive technology that allows them to develop their own "well-being plan." "The center serves as a laboratory where people can interact, reflect, and draw their own conclusions as to the best means to achieve lifelong well-being," noted Raja Rajamannar, senior vice president and chief innovation and marketing officer.

The Innovation Center brings together Humana's clinical leadership, database information, technology, and consumer research in a powerful way to strengthen the connection between the company's products and its members, and to shift the emphasis from illness to wellness. The Innovation Center advances product development, clinical strategy, and support services; gathers research on medical developments, treatment outcomes, and consumer behavior; invests in data analytics that help predict future illnesses; and designs clinical and wellness interventions to prevent them.

"Innovation is very purposeful, disciplined, and process-oriented," said Rajamannar. "It's about creating new concepts, products, and services that satisfy today's needs—and coming up with useful technologies that people haven't imagined yet, that give us a competitive edge in the marketplace. Who had the need for an iPod until an iPod came along?"

Since consumers formed the heart of Humana's new strategy, the first order of business at the Innovation Center was to better understand what consumers want, how they interact with the health care system, and how they make decisions. Humana hired market researchers from leading consumer firms such as Procter & Gamble

A REWARDING PURSUIT ///

The associates at Humana believe that small, daily efforts to live a healthy lifestyle will add up for its members. In 2011, Humana took the next logical step in promoting wellness: rewarding members for improving and maintaining good health. Humana formed a joint venture with South Africa–based Discovery Holdings to offer the firm's Vitality Wellness Program in the U.S. under the name HumanaVitality. Jack Lamon (left), a project manager for Humana Rewards, meets with Rewards analyst Jeremy Milam.

to conduct ethnographic research and coordinate focus groups—a daily routine for consumer product firms, but something that had never been tried by health insurers. In an eighteen-month ethnographic study, researchers followed members home to understand how they managed their health care choices, claims, and budgets so that Humana could figure out how to offer members the relevant information that they needed to make those decisions. Participants created video and written diaries about their doctor visits, online searches for new treatments, and experiences trying to find the best hospital for specific procedures.

One respondent told Humana he almost skipped having an elective surgery because the murky estimates provided by the hospitals indicated the procedure might cost $3,000 out of pocket. The man decided to go

ahead, and found out the out-of-pocket cost was just a few hundred dollars. "This was the best thing I've ever done for myself . . . and I almost decided not to have it," the agitated member said on the video. That finding inspired Humana to build an online search tool so consumers can compare hospitals based on their average discounted price for treating an illness from beginning to end, as well as compare pharmacy costs.

The ethnographers also noticed that many of the participants never used Humana's online tools in choosing and using their health plans. Some didn't have computer access at home; others thought they would have to print everything out and were concerned about the cost of ink. In response, Humana set up interactive kiosks at the offices of some of its larger employer-customers during open enrollment.

MOVE

FREEDOM

ON THE BALL ///

Associates who work out of Humana's Innovation Center are constantly on the lookout for ways to improve the "four pillars of well-being": health, security, belonging, and purpose. Gaming is one of the ways that they see opportunities for engaging consumers in improved wellness. Shane Regala, an analyst for consumer innovation, tests a prototype—a Pac-Man video game controlled by an exercise ball—for integrating core strength into gaming.

In addition, bringing all of its disciplines together in one Innovation Center gave Humana the opportunity to better leverage and integrate its diverse capabilities to provide comprehensive care. For example, the company had always offered excellent disease and care-management programs, as well as a popular 800-number service called HumanaFirst, through which members could speak with a registered nurse. But the two divisions functioned in self-contained silos. Callers with questions related to cardiac disease were not identified as potential candidates for Humana's cardiac-related disease management programs. In 2001, Humana contracted with CareWise, a new vendor, to provide triage services for Humana members and help connect them to the company's clinical and care management resources. Now a caller with a cardiac-related question who is eligible for one of Humana's disease management programs will be referred for follow-up and support.

MINING DATA TO PROMOTE HEALTH AND WELLNESS

A critical component of Humana's wellness strategy was to reach out proactively to customers and position itself as an infomediary by leveraging its massive database. "We are here to help people get a better deal in the health care system because we know what's happening with people across the system. We see their interactions with all the players and can bring the educational component," McCallister said. "We give people good help and guide them to the right places. But we were beginning to think we could do something more, tied to actual health and wellness versus only health solutions."

While protecting members' privacy, the company is uniquely positioned to aggregate, analyze, and draw insights from data that arrives from every point in the system: hospitals, pharmacies, laboratories, doctors, and specialty providers. From these insights, consumers can be empowered to change behavior. Bruce Goodman, senior vice president and chief service and information officer, spearheaded the technology transformation. "In predictive modeling we capture what we call 'the exhaust' from different transactions—claims, diagnosis, lab reports—and that goes into a data warehouse," he said. "It collects lots of data, and then people using advanced tools can go in there, analyze data, and predict who would be a good candidate for intervention so they don't wind up with a health problem—and intervene so people who already have a condition can avoid a repeat hospitalization."

Humana is uniquely positioned to manage health care information, said Tom Liston, senior vice president, senior products. "The volume of data about health care and medical science triples every three-and-a-half years, so it's unmanageable for any practitioner to keep up with best methods," Liston explained. "Humana is gathering that information and creating tools for consumers so they can apply the best-known methods to their individual situations and get the best care at the lowest cost appropriate for the situation. That doesn't happen in the delivery system now because people aren't paid right and people don't know what questions to ask, so people default to 'more is better.'

"We want to figure out what are the preventive things we will pay for now to save larger costs down the road," Liston continued. "For example, there is a lot of unnecessary back surgery. We want to reach out and say, 'Did you know your treatment alternatives range from stretching, which will cost zero, to surgery, which will cost $4,000, and the chances of having a second surgery after the first is 48 percent? Here are all the questions you should be asking the surgeon before your treatment.' So members are confident when they walk

A REASSURING VOICE ///

Participants in the Humana
Cares program receive
personal guidance either
from personal health
consultants or Humana Cares
managers who are licensed
nurses or social services
providers, depending on their
needs. These clinical and
non-clinical professionals
help coordinate care for
members with chronic
conditions, brainstorming
solutions from transportation,
education, and prescription
needs to how to make the
return home from a hospital
stay less stressful. Far left:
Kimberley Byrnes Davis, RN,
speaks with a Humana Cares
member. Near left: Savi
Lenis, a clinical pharmacy
consultant, discusses a
member referral.

into the doctor's office, and they are ready to have a good conversation and come to a more informed decision. Most people will try something less invasive before they go to the most extreme therapy."

Most important, being in the center of the data flow gives Humana powerful tools to assist members in achieving well-being. "When we sign someone up, we do a health risk assessment and collect data. Then they go to physicians, have things done, get lab tests," Liston said. "We're learning more about the person as we process all their claims. What we are moving toward, which I think is incredibly exciting, is to apply clinical algorithms to that data in real time to show the person we understand them, we are applying the best known clinical knowledge to their situation, and reaching out to let them know there's something they could or should do."

Using its vast data trove, Humana decided to reach out to customers with actionable health and coverage information to help them take charge of their well-being. At its simplest, empowerment means using

claims data to identify members who have not had a preventive test in a recommended time period for their age group, such as a mammogram or colonoscopy, and using voice application technology to send a phone call reminder to set up an appointment. "Addressing gaps in care is very important," said Goodman. "If a member is diabetic, we know from the data the last time he or she had an eye or foot exam or HbA1c blood test done. We can send them a message that says, 'It's been over a year and it's important to have your foot examined.' For people taking prescriptions, if you want, we can remind you on your smart phone that it's time to take your pill." Similar technology is employed in Humana's "Maximize Your Benefit" program launched in 2005, which automatically calls members to let them know when a lower-cost, therapeutically equivalent prescription drug is available so they can save money.

In fact, one prescription plan member credited Humana with saving her life. She had been prescribed new medications to help with her fibromyalgia and

depression. The patient filled one month's worth of the three medications at a local pharmacy and sent off the remainder of the prescription to RightSource, Humana's mail order prescription drug business. But upon taking the first week's worth of the new medications, the member started experiencing severe vomiting, hallucinations, abdominal pain, and headaches. She called her doctor's office and was told those were normal side effects. Over the course of the next week, the symptoms grew worse, and she had a seizure. The patient called the doctor's office and was again assured the side effects were normal and eventually the symptoms should subside. Later that day, her phone rang and it was a pharmacist from RightSource. He had received her prescriptions and told her that combining those three medications could be fatal, as they all contained high dosages of serotonin. The member explained her symptoms to him, and he recommended that she go to the hospital and receive care immediately.

The member was diagnosed with serotonin syndrome and spent two weeks in the intensive care unit while doctors worked to rid her body of the critically high levels of these drugs. She recovered and returned home, and credits the RightSource pharmacist—and Humana's sophisticated prescription tracking system—for her outcome.

At its most complex, empowerment means using predictive modeling techniques to identify members at risk of developing certain diseases or chronic conditions so they can change their behavior and prevent the illness. According to the Centers for Disease Control and Prevention (CDC), seven out of ten deaths in the United States occur because of chronic conditions, including heart disease, stroke, cancer, and diabetes. They are among the most common, costly, and preventable of all health problems in the U.S. The CDC has found that four modifiable health risk behaviors—lack of physical activity, poor nutrition, tobacco use, and excessive alcohol consumption—are responsible for much of the illness, suffering, and early deaths related to chronic diseases. The Humana database analysis looks for individuals whose demographics, health history, and lifestyle choices put them at risk for developing or worsening these conditions and reaches out to them with resources to improve their quality of life, to build their knowledge and confidence as health consumers, and to help them reduce cost.

Liston gave the example of a member who has had a heart attack: "We can look in their pharmacy file and see they haven't gotten their beta blocker prescription drug filled. Independent clinical authorities, including Johns Hopkins, say that most people who have a heart attack should take a beta blocker to prevent a second heart attack. We'll send a message to the member to talk with their doctor about it and let them know that we will cover all but five dollars of that drug. That's a win-win. It helps the consumer stay healthy and not have another heart attack, which might cost $50,000. We have to focus our efforts in the early stages and be willing to pay for extra things that are good for people and build that trust over time. We have to get the right things done early before someone progresses to the stage when they have to go into a hospital. Any time patients have to go in a hospital that's a failure on our part."

In addition, Humana mines the claims data of qualifying Medicare members to predict which seniors are at risk for a fall, including people taking medicines that cause dizziness and those who use canes or walkers. Falls are the leading cause of injury and injury-related death for people sixty-five and older, and cost $19 billion in 2000, according to the CDC. That number is expected to rise to nearly $55 billion by 2020 as the population ages. Of those who fall, 20 to 30 percent suffer injuries that decrease mobility and independence.

Humana works with seniors to review their situation and living environment to mitigate common fall risks. For example, a seventy-nine-year-old member quit physical therapy because it was too exhausting. Consequently she became weaker and was at greater risk for falls. A Humana team helped her sign up to get physical therapy at home to help her build her strength and to reduce her risk of falling. In another case, Humana case workers assisted a couple who were both suffering from illnesses by installing grab bars and arranging items more accessibly in their home so they could stay in their own home as long as possible.

"Initially, information technology was a glass-walled data center buried in the basement of a corporation," said Goodman. "Very few people had contact with it. The evolution has been to bring what was once inside that glass house out to the end-users. We're in a very good position to help people take better care of themselves and assist people in lifelong well-being."

Humana is continually refining its technology to get critical data in front of its members. For example, Project Eagle, a desktop application rolled out in 2010, provides customer care specialists with a comprehensive view of members when they call with a service question. The landing page gives service representatives an on-screen view of the member's recent claims and contact history. For example, a member may call about a claim that has been denied. "We can see immediately that their coordination of benefits information is out of date, or whatever the issue may be," said Billy Spegal, production team lead. More important, Project Eagle allows Humana to transform a transactional call into a health guidance opportunity. Algorithms bounce off the data engine and tell the service representative if the person is a good candidate for one of Humana's clinical programs or its personal nurse program, based on recent claims.

**EFFICIENT
AND EFFECTIVE ///**

Humana's RightSource
pharmacy operation
provides savings to
members through the
efficiencies afforded by
a streamlined mail-
order operation. Quality
assurance is a top priority
within the automated
dispensing system—and
a reflection of Humana's
longtime commitment
to finding ways to use
innovations to boost
both efficiency and
effectiveness.

"For example, we can see if they have been recently diagnosed with diabetes and steer them into a program that will help them to better manage the disease and become healthier," said Spegal. "The data may show that this person has a lot of claims around a particular condition, and we can see if they need help getting a better doctor, or more understanding about the medications they take. We can not only address questions but provide guidance that will maximize their benefits and move them toward preventive health. We

get a proactive view of who that member is, and it really builds rapport."

In addition, the desktop application contains the latest medical and coverage information to use around a specific disease. If a service representative sees that someone was recently diagnosed with diabetes, the representative can let that person know what to expect in terms of coverage for insulin and other treatment-related needs so he can better navigate his insurance and maximize his benefits. Project Eagle also contains "guidance alerts" that let the customer care specialist know if the person is a candidate for a preventive health test or procedure, such as a vision screening, mammogram, colonoscopy, or cholesterol check.

INCENTIVES TO REWARD HEALTHY BEHAVIOR

In 2011, Humana took the next logical step in promoting wellness: rewarding members for improving and maintaining good health. Humana formed a joint venture with South Africa–based Discovery Holdings to offer the firm's Vitality Wellness Program in the U.S. Vitality is recognized as one of the world's best programs in motivating and rewarding healthier living. Discovery took a 25 percent stake in the new venture, called HumanaVitality.

"This joint venture fits perfectly with Humana's consumer-focused strategy that integrates health, wellness, and lifelong well-being as our platform for future growth," said McCallister. "It also unites Discovery's wellness expertise and ability to integrate health and well-being solutions with rewards and Humana's demonstrated innovation in consumer engagement that fosters positive behavior change."

Discovery Vitality, an international brand, is the world's largest incentive-based health-enhancement program, serving more than 1.9 million people

EAGLE-EYED FOCUS
ON RELATIONSHIPS ///

The Project Eagle desktop application, rolled out in 2010, provides tools for customer service representatives to tailor each telephone interaction with members to offer personalized health guidance. Left: Billy Spegal demonstrates a sample Project Eagle landing page using a fictitious member's information. Opposite: Ayleen Butz, customer care specialist, takes inbound calls to address and resolve member questions and concerns.

worldwide. Discovery's U.S. subsidiary, the Vitality Group, covers more than 120,000 people and includes a distribution agreement with Wellness & Prevention, a Johnson & Johnson company. The Vitality Group offers large U.S.-based employers access to 8,000 health clubs, 2,500 retail partners for health screenings, and an online mall where members can use reward points to purchase more than 600,000 items.

In July 2011, Vitality's rewards programs will be integrated into the Project Eagle platform. "The future will be rewarding consumers for behaviors around preventive screenings and really driving healthier outcomes," said Spegal. "Points can be leveraged in a mall where you can get an iPod, or if you really go all out, maybe accumulate enough points to get a trip somewhere. There will be a wide range of incentives to reward those behaviors."

Discovery has demonstrated quantifiable success in changing people's behavior and lowering the economic costs of chronic illness. In 2010 alone, the program provided its members with more than 500,000 flights, nearly 20,000 hotel stays, and 3.5 million movie tickets for meeting lifestyle modification goals. Over the last ten years, this has given Discovery the lowest health-cost trend in the marketplace. Recently published research shows that Vitality members also have lower health care costs and lower rates of hospital admission than the general population. The science-based wellness solution is built on a comprehensive integrated approach to lifestyle, focusing on physical activity, education, screening, tobacco-cessation, and nutrition.

A SMART STATEMENT TO SMILE ABOUT ///

In addition to providing in-person guidance and support to members in a way that fosters well-being, Humana has sought ways to empower members to understand their own medical records and spending. The SmartSummary statement, opposite, provides clear communications about payments as well as health care advice tailored to the member's needs. Right: Debbie Sanders, coordinator at the Zephyrhills Guidance Center, shares a hug with member Samantha Sykes.

PERSONALIZED COMMUNICATION_____

In addition to analyzing data to improve members' health, Humana tapped its consumer research findings to vastly improve its communications with members. It introduced SmartSummary and SmartSummary Rx, the industry's first cumulative, personalized cost and benefits statement that shows Humana members what doctors they saw, what prescriptions they filled, how much they paid for them, and how to save money in the future. The four- to eight-page full-color booklet replaces the old explanation of benefits (EOB) statement with its spare technical language and cryptic treatment codes. SmartSummary not only clarifies medical spending but also empowers people to manage their own medical records.

"We spent a lot of time with the consumer, figuring out what would be useful to them," said McCallister. "We needed to produce a report that looks like the rest of their lives. For example, their credit card bill shows them how they started the month, where they spent, and how they finished the month. Our statement says, 'Here's what you did economically relative to health care—here's what you paid and here's what we paid the doctor,' and then because of that they have a broader view. Clinically, if they are taking drug A, we tell them they can save money and get the same result if they use drug B, and to ask their doctor about it."

Chris Nicholson, a director in Humana's strategic communications organization, was on a plane when his elderly seatmate brought up the topic of health insurance and began raving about the SmartSummary statement, pulling out her own copy to show him, according to *Insurance and Technology* magazine. When Nicholson told the retired schoolteacher that he worked for the firm, she said she planned to stay with Humana because of the quality of information she received. In fact, she carried her SmartSummary Rx document with her at all times because it described the drugs she was taking, and she felt it could potentially save her life in an emergency.

Humana mailed its first edition of SmartSummary in October 2005 to a group that included 17,000 Humana associates and followed up with surveys to collect members' feedback. The pilot program helped the company to plan for call center staffing and to anticipate the kind of questions it was likely to receive, which in turn helped the firm prepare for a broader rollout in January 2006.

SmartSummary has become an important tool in retaining Medicare customers. After the initial release, Humana experienced a 14 percent increase in members who said they would stay with Humana based on the types of communications they receive, and a 17 percent increase in respondents who said they would recommend the plan. Better information is also good business, said Goodman: "To the extent that the document gives a member or provider necessary information so they don't have to make a phone call or go to the web, we've saved money by doing that as well."

SmartSummary is fully customized for Humana plan members. The statement starts with a table

of contents, explains medical activity, and features personalized messages about potential cost savings. The statement also includes personalized drug information, relevant articles on medical topics, coupons specific to the member's health needs, and in the case of SmartSummary Rx, vital information about regular prescriptions, including full-color illustrations of pills and refill schedules. SmartSummary Rx also offers a pocket guide with a folding document that seniors can cut out to list their drugs. In 2006, SmartSummary received a Stevie Award for Best New Product from the American Business Awards.

We are committed to creating a smooth administrative experience by paying claims quickly and accurately the first time. Our goal is to have physicians continue to say that Humana is the easiest company to do business with in the industry.

—BRUCE PERKINS

SENIOR VICE PRESIDENT OF HEALTH CARE DELIVERY SYSTEMS AND CLINICAL PROCESSES

CONSUMERISM 2.0

The customized health tips in the SmartSummary report are part of a broader effort by Humana's Innovation Center to increase the focus on enhancing healthier lifestyles rather than simply treating illness. "We felt 2009 a good time to step back and take a fresh look at our strategic direction, resulting in the expansion of our strategic horizons to embrace an invigorating new dream—to help people achieve lifelong well-being," the 2009 annual report stated.

As a core component of the wellness strategy, the Innovation Center launched Humana Games for Health (HG4H) with a mission to design, develop, and research video games that become a catalyst for good health—for members of all ages. "Besides developing original games for health, the Humana Games for Health team looks to partner with game developers who are open to new business models to offer unique video games that can improve health and wellness," said Rajamannar.

For example, in 2009 Humana partnered with a game developer to design a version of the exercise and fitness game Dancetown for seniors. Players dance on a pad that has nine 12" x 12" squares, while graphics on a television screen guide the dancer's movements to the music. The steps become more complex and frequent as the dancer improves. After each dance, the dancer gets feedback on the number of correct steps and her overall score. The program also offers a web-based system for recording a player's performance and tracking progress over time. A Dancetown player (or her family or medical professional) can see at a glance how her dancing is progressing daily, weekly, and monthly. In addition to being in six of its Guidance Centers, Dancetown is also available for purchase by businesses that cater to the senior population.

Humana invited healthy residents between the ages of sixty-seven and eighty-eight from three assisted living facilities to try out the program twice a week for twelve weeks. Participants said the game improved their ability to climb stairs, walk longer distances, and get things done around the house. The activity also reduced feelings of anxiety and depression. "Dancetown was a great fit, enabling us to offer an activity for seniors that impacts all three aspects of well-being: mental, physical, and social," said Rajamannar. The company subsequently installed the game in six of its Humana Guidance Centers.

For more frail seniors, Humana is testing innovative monitoring technology. In a 2011 partnership with Intel,

PLAY THAT IS
SERIOUS BUSINESS ///

Humana Games for Health
(HG4H), the team within
Humana's Innovation Center
that focuses on video
games as a component of
an overall wellness strategy,
has partnered with game
developers to tailor games to
members' needs. One fitness
game, Dancetown, left, has
been adapted for seniors
by the HG4H team and
placed in six of Humana's
Guidance Centers.

Humana Cares launched a pilot program to monitor one thousand high-risk patients across the country using the Intel Health Guide—telemetric monitoring equipment offering real-time health status updates. A member could, for example, step on a special scale at home, and the results would be transmitted over the Internet to a nurse's work station, allowing for immediate follow-up in the event of a health setback. Other bracelet-like monitoring devices are being tested that remotely link an elderly person to his or her adult children, who can receive text messages informing them of their parent's status. Humana also formed a joint venture with Swiss medical device maker Card Guard to design a cell phone–based diabetes-monitoring program, which transmits results wirelessly to medical professionals.

Another innovative program supports members who have recently been released from the hospital. Humana's "Well Dine" program delivers meals to eligible Medicare Advantage members after an inpatient stay at a medical facility. The member receives up to ten frozen, precooked, nutritious meals delivered by Well Dine at no charge, along with a guide on healthy eating. Well Dine has served more than one million meals to more than 81,000 Humana members since the program began in 2006. The program was inspired by studies showing that Medicare members in their first few days at home are often vulnerable to readmission, in part because of challenges with food preparation. Humana Medicare Advantage members who participate in the Well Dine program have fewer hospital readmissions, shorter hospital stays, and fewer emergency room visits.

A WIDER COMMUNITY IMPACT

Humana recognized it could move beyond its own membership with innovations that make an impact on an entire community. Inspired by successful programs in Europe, in 2007 the Innovation Center began testing a bike-sharing program at its Louisville headquarters to give Humana's associates a healthy and green transportation alternative.

HUMANA /// TODAY

**EXTENDING
WELLNESS INTO THE
GOLDEN YEARS ///**

Humana offers
SilverSneakers exercise
classes at its Guidance
Centers throughout
the country. The
program, which provides
conditioning classes and
other fun and energizing
activities for older adults,
is aimed at helping
members take greater
control of their health and
improving their strength,
balance, flexibility, and
endurance.

MAKING HEALTH FUN AND FUN HEALTHY ///

Humana has explored the benefits of bike riding—both for members and the environment—though a variety of programs. Its bike-sharing program called "Freewheelin" is available at some Guidance Centers, where bikes as well as support are offered to members interested in getting out on the road. Right top: Members Maxine Thompson, Joanne Young, and Sandy Cooper leave the Zephyrhills, Florida, Guidance Center for a group ride. Right bottom: Celia Conti, the safety education and bike liaison for the Zephyrhills group, pulls a bike out for a member.

That successful pilot program developed into a bike-sharing program called "Freewheelin", in partnership with Bikes Belong, a cycling advocacy organization, and a variety of municipalities.

"As a health-benefits company, we are honored to have a role in introducing Americans to bike-sharing, a concept which has long been popular overseas and has proven that individuals can easily integrate healthy living and environmental conservation into their lives," said Rajamannar. "The potential for this program is tremendous, as it provides answers to some of the most

difficult public health problems facing our nation—how to improve personal and environmental health while at the same time reducing costs."

Freewheelin provided one thousand free bicycles for the 2008 Democratic and Republican national conventions in Denver and Minneapolis-St. Paul. The result: 7,523 bike rides; 41,724 miles ridden; 1.3 million calories burned; and 14.6 metric tons of carbon offset. In fall 2009, Humana installed permanent eighteen-bike Freewheelin stations at three Guidance Centers in Nevada, Arizona, and Florida. The stations are open to anyone ages eighteen and up, and free for all community members to use as long as riders present a valid photo ID and credit card.

Buoyed by the success of Freewheelin, Humana introduced B-cycle, a stand-alone business in partnership with Trek Bicycle and Crispin Porter + Bogusky. B-cycle began setting up stations in communities, campuses, and workplaces across the country, with locations in six major cities established by early 2011. Its next-generation bicycles are equipped with computers to track mileage, calories burned, and carbon offsets. Riders can monitor their personal fitness, see their contributions to the city's green efforts, and connect with others online at www.Bcycle.com. In Chicago, for example, the bikes cost ten dollars an hour up to a maximum of forty dollars per day to rent, or fifty-five dollars for a ninety-day membership. To check out bikes, riders register on the web site or directly at the B-stations. They can return the bikes to any of the fifteen B-cycle rack locations in the city.

Other Humana community initiatives have focused on solutions for the obesity epidemic. In every state, more than 15 percent of adults are obese, and in nine states, more than 30 percent of adults are obese. The medical care costs of obesity in the United States are staggering: the CDC estimates that in 2008 dollars, these costs totaled about $147 billion. In addition, childhood obesity

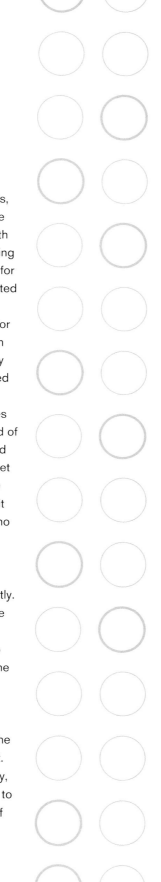

has more than tripled in the past thirty years to nearly 20 percent of children age six to eleven. Humana launched an array of pilot programs to fight obesity, including offering personal coaching and pedometers to consumers, who lost an average of 12.4 pounds each in nine months, and a cell-phone based diet and nutrition program that resulted in an average loss of nine pounds over three months.

The Humana Innovation Center also introduced a video exercise game in 2008 called the Horsepower Challenge, which features pedometers linked to computers. The information on the pedometer is uploaded to a web site with racehorse avatars, which tells participants how many points they earned based on the number of steps they took. Kids can redeem the points to dress up their avatar, buying it a hat, sunglasses, or a shirt. Kids can also see how their entire team performed and collectively use their points to customize a school bus they are racing in. A later version of the software lets kids race around the world and learn about different countries and attractions, such as the Egyptian pyramids. One of the most publicized uses of the program was called the American Horsepower Challenge, sponsored by The Humana Foundation, the company's philanthropic arm. The game allowed 1,600 students and twenty members of Congress to engage in a friendly four-week competition, walking a combined 50,000 miles and burning 2.25 million calories. The Georgia Institute of Technology is continuing to study the ongoing health benefits of the American Horsepower Challenge.

IMPROVING ADMINISTRATION THROUGH TECHNOLOGY AND INCENTIVES

As Humana's strategy shifted toward a consumer-centric model over the last decade, the company sought to engage its other stakeholders in making health care more efficient and affordable. Humana's regional and national networks include more than 670,000 doctors, hospitals, pharmacies, and ancillary providers. In recent years, the company has structured shared-risk incentive plans with doctors in some markets that compensate them for being more efficient and effective with care. In south Florida, for example, members choose a doctor, who is compensated by Humana in several ways.

"There's a primary care payment, which is there for him to pay his nurses and rent," Liston explained. "Then we put money aside in a specialty pool, which is money that will pay specialists' claims, and a hospital pool used to pay hospital claims. If the doctor needs to refer a patient to a specialist or put him in the hospital, he does so, and we pay those claims out of the pools at the end of the month. If there's a shortfall, we pay half the cost and the doctors pay half the cost, and if it's a surplus, we get half and the physician gets half. So the physician's role is to manage utilization, and our role is to get better unit prices with the specialists and hospitals. Physicians who do all the right things in giving good quality preventive care to members get a bonus.

"It changes the dynamic," Liston continued, "because then physicians organize themselves differently. They may have a staff physician whose job is to see five patients a day at their homes and make sure they are taken care of appropriately to avoid the need to go into the hospital. We want to compensate them for doing the right thing, and not for doing a lot of things."

At the same time that Humana is better aligning incentives in the health care industry, the company is developing and disseminating technology that makes the providers' administrative work easier and more efficient. "We need to make those different constituencies happy, take the hassle out of their interactions with us, and try to encourage self-service as much as possible," said chief service and information officer Bruce Goodman.

We need to make those different constituencies happy, take the hassle out of their interactions with us, and try to encourage self-service as much as possible.

—BRUCE GOODMAN
SENIOR VICE PRESIDENT AND CHIEF SERVICE AND INFORMATION OFFICER

While most industries have tapped into the power of technology to streamline administrative tasks, many health provider offices are still in the dark ages, requires patients to fill out reams of paperwork. "About 80 percent of practices in the U.S. have two or fewer doctors, so it's a cottage industry," said Goodman. "Only about 15 to 20 percent of doctors' offices have electronic medical records; most work with paper files and folders and jackets."

In 2001, Humana teamed up with a competitor, Blue Cross and Blue Shield of Florida (BCBSF), to connect all Florida health care professionals with an online portal to manage electronic claims and other daily health plan transactions. The insurance firms formed a separate company, Availity, which offers a standardized, real-time interface to give providers a single, comprehensive view of each patient's health history. The Availity program also facilitates claims processing and HSA administration at physicians' offices. Availity's technology improves administrative efficiencies and replaces paper- and phone-based systems, giving health care providers more time to focus on patients. "We combined the technical resources of both companies to build out the portal capability," Goodman said. "Today, 95 percent of the physicians in the state of Florida and

all of the hospitals use Availity. That would not have been possible with just Humana."

Less than a decade after it was founded, Availity had become one of the largest electronic data interchange clearinghouses in the nation—processing more than 700 million transactions annually for 65,000 organizations—and the most advanced electronic Health Information Network. "If the provider's administrative staff is willing to put in the information immediately, the providers can get paid in real time," said Goodman. "If they don't put everything in, they can still get a cost estimator so they know what to collect from the members before they leave the office."

Newt Gingrich, former Speaker of the House and founder of the Center for Health Transformation, called Availity "one of the best kept secrets in health care. . . . [T]he success that Availity has had in Florida alone, where virtually every doctor and hospital is connected, should be a model for others to follow." In 2011, Humana and BCBSF sponsored an electronic medical records pilot program that is underway in Florida. It was a natural extension of the Availity initiative, Goodman noted, because "health care payers are in a fairly unique position, in terms of having a very good, consolidated view of many of the patients."

In time, Goodman told the *Wall Street Journal*, technology will transform the consumer health care experience: "To get an appointment at a doctor's office you'd go onto the Web . . . and when you show up at the doctor's office, let's say it was your first visit, a lot of information that normally they would ask you for has already been downloaded. In the exam office, there is a monitor, and the doctor has everything in front of him or her. If there is a prescription needed, the doctor can do that electronically and can find out what's the most cost-effective drug for you and make sure you don't have a drug interaction [issue], because you have already had all of your prescription information downloaded. To pay, you have an ID card, or maybe your cell phone, that immediately connects you, and your claim is adjudicated in real time. There is no paperwork."

In 2009, Humana was named easiest insurance company to do business with by the medical journal *Physicians Practice*. The data, derived from a database run by athenahealth, ranks health insurers according to financial and administrative performance and medical policy complexity. The data included more than 18,000 providers, roughly 41 million transactions, and $7 billion in charges. Humana ranked as having the fewest days in accounts receivable. Its score improved 11.5 percent on this measure, dropping from 30.1 in 2007 to 26.65 days in 2008. Additionally, Humana's denial rate ranked the lowest among national health plans. "We are committed to creating a smooth administrative experience by paying claims quickly and accurately the first time," said Bruce Perkins, senior vice president of health care delivery systems and clinical processes. "Our goal is to have physicians continue to say that Humana is the easiest company to do business with in the industry."

Throughout its history, Humana has flourished by riding the wave of change through innovation. "We have been all over the health care system in some form or fashion—we've managed nursing homes and hospitals, doctors and clinics, diagnostic centers, and insurance plans," said McCallister. "And as we moved through time, the truth is that we have always been involved with helping people. We have always had a direct connection to individuals' health and well-being. Somebody has to organize the financing and delivery of health care and help people figure out how to improve their own health and change the way they are using the system, because if we don't change, the cost of taking care of folks is going to overwhelm the nation."

SHARED INFORMATION, BETTER BENEFITS ///

Humana teamed up with another health insurance provider to develop Availity, an industry-wide portal to manage electronic claims and health plan transactions. In addition to making claims processing more efficient, the program also offers providers a comprehensive view of each patient's health history. Former Speaker of the House Newt Gingrich called Availity "one of the best-kept secrets in health care."

05

—
SOCIAL RESPONSIBILITY

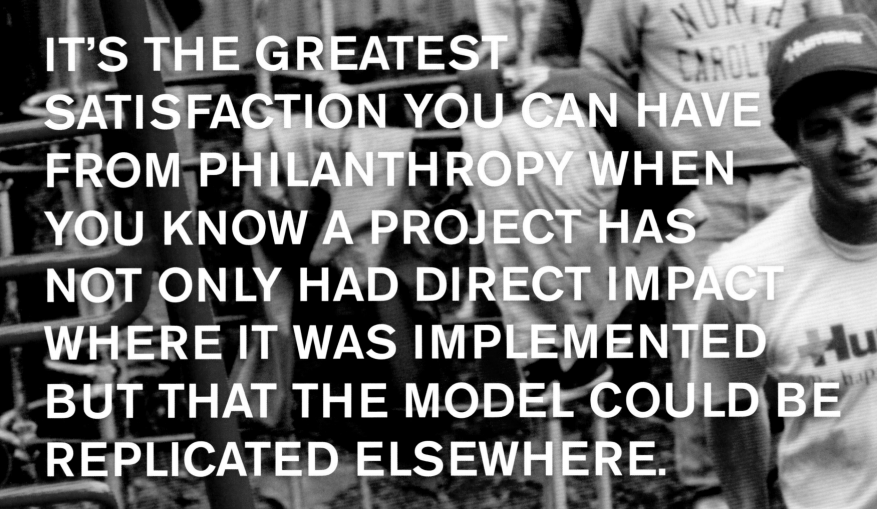

IT'S THE GREATEST SATISFACTION YOU CAN HAVE FROM PHILANTHROPY WHEN YOU KNOW A PROJECT HAS NOT ONLY HAD DIRECT IMPACT WHERE IT WAS IMPLEMENTED BUT THAT THE MODEL COULD BE REPLICATED ELSEWHERE.

—VIRGINIA KELLY JUDD
EXECUTIVE DIRECTOR OF THE HUMANA FOUNDATION

PITCHING IN TO HELP ///
Humana has made it a priority to support associates' own volunteer efforts through The Humana Foundation's Humana Volunteer Network, which provides resources and recognition via an online portal.

HUMANA
Guidance when you need it most

PEDAL-PUSHING ///
B-cycle bikes are lined up
during the launch of the
Denver B-cycle program on
Earth Day in 2010. B-cycle
has set up bike-sharing
stations in communities,
campuses, and workplaces
across the country.

In 1970, seventeen-year-old Bill Baldwin had just graduated from high school in Louisville. A friend told him about an opening in the mailroom at a local company called Extendicare. "I was the lowest man on the totem pole, and I wasn't planning to go to college," said Baldwin, who couldn't afford the tuition. One day his boss, David A. Jones, pulled Baldwin aside. "He offered to pay for my college personally out of his pocket," said Baldwin, who attended the University of Louisville part-time at night while working full-time. He eventually earned not only a bachelor's degree, but two master's degrees, in business and health services administration.

"I felt a large sense of gratitude to Mr. Jones and the company," said Baldwin. "Without the help, I might not have gone to college. Then as the company grew, opportunities presented themselves." Three decades after starting in the mailroom, Baldwin was serving as director of information technology acquisitions for Humana.

Humana later established formal programs to assist associates, and eventually their children, in furthering their education. Since 1991, the program has provided more than $9 million in college scholarships for children of Humana associates. "Everything in life is about people," said Jones. "We had a lot of young people who started with the company who turned out to be bright kids—and Bill is a good example. Given my background, where I couldn't afford to go to college without a scholarship, I was very empathetic, and Humana now has a wonderful program to help with education."

and 2010, the company and The Humana Foundation contributed $220 million to charitable initiatives and community organizations, and leveraged the volunteer efforts of Humana's associates. The foundation has been a critical part of Kentucky's philanthropic network, and through a special sixteen-year project, helped revitalize the health care system in Romania after the fall of the Iron Curtain. In 2008, *Corporate Responsibility* magazine ranked Humana seventh on its list of the one hundred best corporate citizens, a group that includes companies such as Intel, PepsiCo, and Starbucks. Humana was the only health services company to rank in the top twenty.

HONORING ITS KENTUCKY ROOTS

Humana's earliest philanthropic efforts started at home, with contributions to Kentucky's educational, cultural, arts, and civic institutions, as well as a major health care commitment to Louisville's indigent population. In the mid-1970s, the company began supporting the Fund for the Arts and the Louisville Science Center, and in 1976 it started making financial contributions to the Metro United Way. In 1979, Humana funded Actors Theatre of Louisville's Festival of New American Plays for the first time, a commitment that is now the longest-running corporate sponsorship of a performing arts organization in the country. This thriving partnership with Actors Theatre demonstrates a joint commitment to artistic exploration and appreciation at home, across the region, and around the globe.

Jones recalled that even as his family struggled financially in his boyhood, his mother always gave 10 percent of their income to charity. "I don't know why she was so passionate about charity but she was, and we grew up with that," Jones said. "So I learned to share at a time when our resources were meager. But there was a lot of love around, and sharing is a good thing."

Humana has a long history of changing lives through sharing its resources to support education, the arts, civic and cultural institutions, disaster relief efforts, and health and wellness in communities where the company has a meaningful presence. The Humana Foundation was formally established in 1981 and endowed to ensure permanent charitable giving by the company in all economic cycles. Between 1974

Over the last three decades, more than four hundred Humana Festival plays have been produced, representing the work of more than two hundred playwrights. Three plays received Pulitzer Prizes: D. L. Coburn's *The Gin Game*, Beth Henley's *Crimes of the Heart*, and Donald Margulies's *Dinner with Friends*. Six

21ˢᵗ ANNUAL HUMANA FESTIVAL OF NEW AMERICAN PLAYS — MADE POSSIBLE BY A GENEROUS GRANT FROM THE HUMANA FOUNDATION — ACTORS THEATRE OF LOUISVILLE / MARCH 4–APRIL 13, 1997

Humana plays have won the American Theatre Critics Award, four have won Obies, and eight have been adapted for film and television. In 2004, *Variety* magazine acknowledged the Humana Festival as "the leading showcase of new American works for the theatre."

Some 26,000 people attend the five weeks of plays annually, and more than 90 million Americans have seen additional productions of plays originated in the festival, not including film audiences who have seen screen adaptations. Audience members at the festival each year typically represent more than thirty foreign countries.

"Through its active and continuing support of the [festival] for over thirty years, Humana has literally created a generation of writers for the American stage," wrote Jon Jory, the festival's founding director, in a letter to Jones. "Hundreds of playwrights have, through the festival, been brought to the attention of the world theater community, and a majority of the best known began their careers under Humana's banner. Over

two hundred Humana plays have been published, and festival scripts are performed on every continent in dozens of languages. Who could have predicted that Humana would transform American playwriting and be the most important supporter of young writers the business world has ever known?" In 2007, Humana and its foundation received the 2007 Theatre Communications Group Corporate Funder Award for its support of the festival.

A HOME FOR THE ARTS

In 1980, Humana extended its commitment by facilitating the development of a permanent home for the arts in Louisville. Humana cofounder Wendell Cherry spearheaded the construction of the Kentucky Center for the Performing Arts, which opened in 1983. The center, composed of three theaters, is home to the Louisville Orchestra, Kentucky Opera, and Louisville Ballet, as well as a host of community theater performances. It also

A PATRON WITH
PURPOSE ///

Humana cofounder Wendell
Cherry's love of the arts
ignited the health benefits
company's strong support of
arts programs in Louisville.
Cherry, near right, chaired
the board of directors of
the Kentucky Center for the
Performing Arts and donated
several sculptures for
the project, including
Alexander Calder's *The Red
Feather*, far right.

features the Governor's School for the Arts in Louisville, offering intensive training for hundreds of high school students every summer. The center's programming and educational courses bring the arts to children and adults in virtually all of Kentucky's 120 counties.

"Both Mr. Jones and Mr. Cherry had an interest in the performing arts and supported these organizations in many ways," said Charlie Teeple, Humana's former vice president of investor relations and communications. "For years in Louisville there was talk about needing an auditorium for the performing arts—and there was talk and talk and talk until finally Wendell got involved and got it built. They were doers, not talkers. And this activity took place while they were building the company."

Rose Lenihan Rubel served on the center's first board of directors with Cherry. At the initial meeting, Cherry "introduced us to his vision of the center and what it could do for the future of Louisville," Rubel wrote in a book of essays honoring Cherry after his death. "He presented

pages of details about the building and the people who would be employed. He enlisted the help of arts groups and schools, which brought together the community's interests through involvement in the project. What I remember most about working with Wendell was his total dedication to the completion of the project. He often became so engrossed in the project that he would lose track of time. It was not an unusual event to receive a call at midnight or 2:00 a.m. from Wendell telling me to be prepared to fly out of town at dawn to view furnishings for the center. . . . It was an honor to witness such a brilliant, forceful achiever at work. I will always be grateful to him for allowing me to be part of such an important contribution to Louisville."

Under Cherry's supervision, the project was completed on time and on budget, said Jones: "All the significant experience that Wendell had in building several billion dollars worth of hospitals for Humana was brought to bear on the Kentucky Center for the Performing Arts." In addition, Cherry donated significant twentieth

Education is my passion. Education is the passport that allows individuals to climb the ladder. I don't care where you were born or how you started out, education is the most important thing because at the end of the day, all we have as individuals are the skills we possess.

—DAVID A. JONES
COFOUNDER

century works of art for the project, including sculpture by Alexander Calder, John Chamberlain, Jean Dubuffet, Louise Nevelson, Joan Miró, Malcolm Morley, and Tony Smith.

Robert Harris, an architect, worked closely with Cherry on the building's design and construction. "The process of the design and intricacies of building could fill a book," Harris wrote in an essay honoring Cherry after his death. "But after most of the work was complete, Wendell . . . several others, and myself sat in Whitney Hall one morning to hear the first rehearsal. The Louisville Orchestra, on stage for the first time, raised their bows and filled the air with grand music, confirming the acousticians' assumptions, and thus beginning the life of one of Wendell's dreams."

EDUCATIONAL AND HEALTH CARE INITIATIVES IN LOUISVILLE

Meanwhile, Humana facilitated the dreams of young African Americans in Greater Louisville through the YMCA's Black Achievers Program. Since 1980, Humana has contributed more than $690,000 to a program that enhances the educational, personal, and career development of African American youth in grades eight through twelve. The program connects them with more than two hundred adult volunteers, including Humana associates, to help them

establish and pursue their goals. In 2010 Humana was honored with the YMCA's Legacy Award for its thirty years of supporting the Black Achievers Program. Humana also supports the Business Higher Education Forum's College Readiness Initiative, which promotes college readiness, access, and work/life success.

In other local education activities, Humana and its foundation have supported local Junior Achievement programs since 1974, and in partnership with Ashland Inc., Humana formed the Governor's Scholars Program for gifted high school juniors throughout Kentucky. As early as 1983, Humana was putting computers into local schools. In addition, Jones was one of three founders of the Partnership for Kentucky Schools in 1990—a response to the passage of the Kentucky Education Reform Act, one of the most sweeping reforms in the country at the time. The group brings together school communities and the business sector to improve students' academic performance and readiness for work and civic life.

"Education is my passion," said Jones. "Education is the passport that allows individuals to climb the ladder. I don't care where you were born or how you started out, education is the most important thing because at the end of the day, all we have as individuals are the skills we possess. You need to have

A NEW HOME ///

Humana's contributions to Louisville touched even the physical and visual order of the city when, in the early 1980s, the company decided to construct its new headquarters building on Main Street. The twenty-seven-story postmodern tower, designed by renowned architect Michael Graves after a worldwide architectural competition, was completed in 1985 and was awarded the National Honor Award by the American Institute of Architects in 1987. Right: David A. Jones, Michael Graves, and Wendell Cherry at the Humana Building media briefing in June 1985. Opposite: The Humana Building.

the confidence that comes from having skills. If you don't have skills you are always at risk, because the resources that we have, such as stocks, can be wiped out overnight. I want to be helpful without creating dependency so that people can be self-reliant."

In 1982, Humana extended its hometown philanthropy to health care, intervening to solve a major crisis in the city of Louisville. The University of Louisville had decided to stop operating the city's unaccredited and money-losing public hospital. In partnership with local and state government, Humana agreed to lease and operate a new facility called Humana Hospital-University and provide care to local citizens without regard to their ability to pay, which solved the city's indigent care problem. Humana's contract limited cost increases to the lesser of either the city's percentage increase in tax revenues or the consumer price index, an agreement that saved Louisville tens of millions of dollars over the decade that Humana ran the hospital.

RESHAPING THE SKYLINE

In addition to serving the people of Louisville, Humana made a powerful contribution to the urban landscape. In the early 1980s, the company decided to construct

a headquarters building on Main Street that would forever alter the skyline of Louisville and raise the city's international profile. The company held a competition that attracted five renowned architects: Ulrich Franzen, Cesar Pelli, Norman Foster, Helmut Jahn, and Michael Graves.

"We were interested in a design that fit the location, rather than being concerned with a particular style," said Jones. "Our charge to participants in our competition was that they be bold and not feel constrained by any notion of what's proper for Louisville. We provided each of the contestants with a personal walking tour and history of the city. Our goal was to create a functional structure that was environmentally friendly, especially in minimizing the costs of heating, cooling, and maintenance, but which would also inspire and require those creating buildings in the future to think about how their building would relate to its surroundings and to the city."

Humana chose a postmodern tower designed by Michael Graves. The twenty-seven-story structure, totaling 525,000 square feet, is set on an eight-story base of steel and pink granite. An open colonnade of square, deep red granite columns occupies the first few floors and surrounds a fifty-foot entrance waterfall of six cascades, evocative of the Ohio River. The front arcades mimic the height of adjacent structures, providing a smooth contextual fit with the nineteenth century streetscape. The open-air front portion of the loggia also contains a large fountain. The main tower, set well back from the base, is a pink granite building traversed by a shaft of solid glass and small square windows, sloping up, pyramid-like, at the top few floors. The curved top of the building holds an open-air observation deck surrounded by glass, offering majestic views of the Ohio River. A metal truss projects from the building, evoking the nearby river bridges.

**KEEPING HUMANA'S
CHIEF EXECUTIVE
ON TRACK ///**

With his numerous
responsibilities within
Humana and his role in
advocating for innovation
within the health benefits
industry, Mike McCallister
is a busy man. Humana's
chairman and chief
executive officer relies
on a skilled team of
support staff to allow
him to stay focused on
his goal of helping to
"alter the landscape of
health care delivery in the
U.S." Executive assistant
Janice Seaman makes
a note in McCallister's
schedule.

RESHAPING LOUISVILLE ///

RESHAPING LOUISVILLE ///

David A. Jones in front of the Humana Building during its construction. The building was designed with an eye for its placement in the Louisville skyline. Its visual features create a strong transition between the facades of neighboring buildings on both sides. Humana continued to reshape Louisville's urban landscape with multiple renovations and contributions to downtown buildings and parks.

Inside, the front door leads to a beautifully detailed vestibule of different colored pieces of marble, which in turn opens to a square, three-story lobby surrounded by a second-floor arcade; this continues on to a rotunda and the elevator lobbies.

"One reason we selected the Michael Graves design was because of his understanding of the building's location and its environment," said Jones. "The loggias along Main and Fifth streets encourage pedestrians to enjoy the building and stay dry when it rains. The exposed girders reflect the bridges of our river city. The building is oriented toward the river. The front portion of the building is only eight stories high, respecting and transitioning to its lovely cast iron front neighbors to the west. The building also transitions

strongly from its neighbor to the east, using natural materials of marble and granite in contrast to the glass and steel of the neighbor."

In a review of the building in 1985, *New York Times* architecture critic Paul Goldberger wrote: "It is a richly colored composition made up of abstract, highly personal variations on classical forms. It is a kind of collage of modernist and classical elements, put together in a way that is like neither the modernist skyscrapers of the post–World War II years nor the classical skyscrapers of the early years of this century. . . . Humana is a warm and inviting building, perhaps the first skyscraper of our time to be both serious and visually alive. . . . It is at once a building of great dignity and a building of great energy and passion. . . . Humana is a remarkable achievement—in every way Mr. Graves's finest building."

The American Institute of Architects awarded the Humana Building the National Honor Award in 1987, and *Time* magazine named it one of the ten best buildings of the decade. In a 2007 interview with a local publication, Louisville Mayor Jerry Abramson said, "The Humana Building changed architecture, it changed Michael Graves, and it changed the landscape of our city."

Humana continued making an impact on the city's landscape, putting its fundraising muscle behind the Waterfront Development Corporation (WDC), a partnership of city, county, and state government entities dedicated to revitalizing the waterfront. Before the WDC was created in 1986, Louisville's downtown waterfront area—from the Ohio River south to Main Street and between the Clark Memorial and Kennedy Bridges—was one of the most unattractive parts of the city, filled with abandoned or underutilized land and buildings. In 1993, Jones led a private campaign to raise $14.5 million for the Louisville Waterfront Park,

The thing I am most proud of in building Humana is the many good jobs we've helped create. Both Wendell and I had a philosophy that if we created the conditions that allowed people to do their best work, things would work out well for everybody; that's what we still do at Humana.

—DAVID A. JONES
COFOUNDER

with $3.25 million contributed by Humana and its foundation. The park has improved the quality of life of Louisville residents and has also been a catalyst for business and residential redevelopment in the Waterfront District and connecting areas of downtown Louisville. Today Waterfront Park attracts more than 1.5 million visitors every year for festivals, concerts, charity walks, picnics, weddings, and everyday usage—walkers, joggers, and families enjoying the playgrounds. In 2006, it was named one of the Top Ten Urban Parks in the nation by the Urban Land Institute.

But perhaps Humana's most significant local contribution has been its role as the catalyst for Louisville's health care-related economy—the area's largest business sector, according to University of Louisville economists. By 2009, Louisville was home to 2,900 health-related companies and 85,000 health care workers who collectively draw an annual payroll of $3.5 billion. More than four hundred of those businesses were founded locally, many of them by veterans of Humana. Of the twenty-five largest employers in the metropolitan area, ten are health-related businesses, and of the eight Fortune 1000 companies in Kentucky, three are in health care and two are headquartered in Louisville—Humana and Kindred. The Health Enterprises Network, an affiliate

of Greater Louisville Inc., was formed by business leaders in 2000 and is charged with promoting the growth of Louisville's health-related economy.

"The thing I am most proud of in building Humana is the many good jobs we've helped create," said Jones. "Both Wendell and I had a philosophy that if we created the conditions that allowed people to do their best work, things would work out well for everybody; that's what we still do at Humana."

THE ROMANIAN ASSISTANCE PROJECT

In the late 1980s, the philanthropic efforts of Humana and its foundation extended well beyond Kentucky. After the Iron Curtain fell in 1989, President George H. W. Bush reached out to American business leaders to help revive the moribund economies of Eastern Europe. In February 1990, President Bush called Jones, who recruited his friend Boone Powell, Jr., president and chief executive officer of the Baylor Health Care System in Dallas. The two men chose to focus their efforts on the health care system in Romania, which was close to collapse after nearly a quarter century of brutal dictatorship under Nicolae Ceaușescu.

Jones and Powell made an initial visit to Romania in September 1990, accompanied by a ten-member

expert medical team. The group was overwhelmed by what they witnessed at Fundeni Hospital, the largest general hospital in Bucharest. "Many of the walls had large cracks, and the whole place had an air of poverty and neglect," noted Jones in a book published by Humana about the Romanian effort. "The energetic and helpful director of the hospital apologized for these conditions, explaining there had been an earthquake. We later learned there had indeed been an earthquake, but it had occurred many years before. As we made rounds with the director of the cardiovascular surgery department, Dr. Pop de Popa, we noticed that as we left a room, its light bulb was removed and installed in the next room to be visited. Not only was the hospital short of light bulbs, it was short of everything, including aspirin, antibiotics, nurses, cleaning supplies, paint, and equipment of every kind."

In addition, Western medical literature had been banned by the Ceauşescu regime twenty years earlier, and many simple diagnostic and therapeutic techniques were unknown. Nursing schools had been closed for more than a decade. Patients were crowded ten to twelve in a room. Modern equipment was often inoperable because of a lack of spare parts. Despite the absence of resources and technology, Romanian doctors had developed impressive clinical skills along with creative solutions to care for very sick patients. Surgeons who had no regular sutures had them made out of components of shoelaces; heart valves were created from the valves of wild boar caught in hunting expeditions.

Between 1990 and 2006, Humana and Baylor sponsored a dedicated group of volunteer physicians, surgeons, nurses, technology experts, English-language teachers, librarians, and hospital and foundation directors to assess and meet the needs of the Romanian health care system under the auspices of the Romanian Assistance Project. Targeted areas included ophthalmology, pediatrics, nursing, oncology, public health, cardiovascular health, medical information services, and laboratory services. Humana dedicated $11 million over the course of the project to cover travel and living expenses.

Virginia Kelly Judd, executive director of The Humana Foundation, visited Romania twenty-five times between 1991 and 2006. "The emphasis of the project was to create bilateral exchanges and fill information gaps," said Judd. "There was a USAID [United States Agency for International Development] grant of $3 million to supplement what we did, and we established two surgical centers in two hospitals there, bringing sophisticated equipment and supplies." Dr. Allan Lansing, a retired heart surgeon and former chairman of the Humana Heart Institute International in Louisville, served as director of the Cardiovascular Surgery Program of the Romanian Assistance Project and helped set up the two centers.

The team discovered other difficult challenges in pediatric care. In 1966, the Ceaușescu regime, in an attempt to boost the country's population, had introduced new policies to increase the birth rate. Abortion was permitted only in cases where the woman in question was more than forty-two years of age, or was already the mother of four (and later five) children. The orphanage population swelled as parents abandoned newborns they couldn't afford to feed. The state-run institutions were overcrowded and understaffed, failing to meet even the most basic needs of the children. Moreover, a policy of providing blood transfusions to babies to boost their immune systems created an epidemic of pediatric HIV/AIDS, since the blood was untested and syringes were reused.

A Baylor physician and blood-banking specialist, Dr. Alain Marengo-Rowe, arranged for an epidemiologist from Romania to spend time at the Centers for Disease Control and Prevention in Atlanta to train in blood center management. Abbott Laboratories and Humana donated equipment to properly analyze blood. These efforts soon brought blood-banking in Romania to near best-practice standards and led to earlier diagnoses and more precise treatment. A Humana-sponsored volunteer, Dr. George Rodgers, "adopted" each of the nation's eleven pediatric hospitals to help raise standards of care and education.

Over the course of the sixteen-year project, 320 American volunteer medical and technical professionals traveled to Romania, and 340 professionals from Romania traveled to the U.S. for training. Romania reopened its School of Nursing, and the Americans promoted team-centered care in Romania, incorporating nurses as active team members. Some thirty-five American nurse educators trained more than 4,500 Romanian nurses in infectious diseases in three quarters of Romania's counties. The project introduced new pediatric diagnostic and therapeutic techniques in subspecialty areas such as neonatology, oncology, and rheumatology. It established the first hospital-based clinical psychology practitioners program. Cardiac mortality rates declined significantly because volunteer surgeons introduced the coronary bypass procedure, which had been relatively unknown in Romania. Heart surgeries for young children have quadrupled since 1997, and infant mortality rates declined 29 percent over a decade.

Jones said he was overwhelmed by the generosity of volunteers. "Every participant in the project was a volunteer; that was tremendous," said Jones. "We have many doctors who earn $10,000 or more per week who gave up several weeks to go train

HUMANA IN ROMANIA ///

In 1990, after the fall of the Iron Curtain and at the special request of President George H. W. Bush, David A. Jones recruited his longtime friend Boone Powell to join him in an effort to rebuild the health care system in Romania. Over the next sixteen years, the two would transform the Romanian health care system from impoverishment and disaster into a place of "achievement, inspiration, and hope." Opposite left: Jones (far right) and Powell (fifth from left) leading the Romanian Assistance Project's first medical team in Bucharest, September 1990. Opposite right: Jones visiting a Bucharest orphanage as part of the project's first trip to Romania. Below: The medal of the Order of Merit, the highest civilian honor in Romania, which was awarded to Jones and Dr. Allan Lansing by the president of Romania in 2003.

Romanian doctors. Their remarkable generosity has given me the clearest understanding of the desire of people to help other people." He recalled a county manager and computer expert, Kevin McAdams, who initially went over to Romania to solve a specific technical problem and continued to go every year during his vacation to help set up modern medical libraries. Jones offered to speak to his boss to help McAdams get some time off for his volunteer work without using up his vacation days. "He said, 'Well then it wouldn't be my gift. I want to use my time,'" Jones recalled. "I was touched by that and still am."

After sixteen years, The Humana Foundation decided the best way to continue its work was to share the successful public-private partnership model it helped establish in Romania. The foundation board approved a $1 million grant to the University of Louisville for an endowment in pediatrics, which was matched by David and Betty Jones. The university then applied to the state and secured $2 million in additional matching funds. "It was the right moment to step back and let our Romanian partners take charge, and to go forth and share the model," said Judd. "The result is that the program has now gone into a half-dozen other countries, including Vietnam, Africa, and South America, and has been replicated in some way. It's the greatest satisfaction you can have from philanthropy when you know a project has not only had direct impact where it was implemented but that the model could be replicated elsewhere." In 2003, Jones and Dr. Allan Lansing were awarded the Order of Merit by the president of Romania, the nation's highest civilian honor. In 2007, the Council on Foundations gave Humana its Critical Impact Award for its work in Romania.

In a book commemorating the Romanian Assistance Project, President George H. W. Bush wrote: "What had been in 1990 a country whose health care system was both dispirited and dispiriting, was by 2006 transformed into a place of achievement, innovation, and hope, due in part to the Romanian Assistance Project."

Humana's other international efforts have focused on disaster relief. The company, its associates, and the foundation provided more than $2.7 million in emergency funds for communities devastated by earthquakes in Haiti and China in 2010 and 2008, respectively; for Hurricane Katrina victims in 2005; and for people affected by the Asian tsunami in 2004.

SUPPORTING ASSOCIATES' EFFORTS

Just as it buttressed the heroic efforts of volunteers in Romania, The Humana Foundation decided it could make a greater impact at home by doing the same for its own associates. Through the Humana Volunteer Network (HVN), the company and the foundation provide support, resources, and recognition for associates committed to volunteer service. "About three years ago we recognized that associates around the country were volunteering in their communities, but we weren't capturing that information and reporting it out to associates," said Judd. "So we developed HVN, which is a way for associates to go online, create a profile, and enter that data and give us a way to report annually to everyone the good works that they are doing year in and year out. Also, if someone wants to find a volunteer opportunity they can go to the network."

Humana volunteers are given the chance to win a $4,000 "Dollars for Doers" grant for the nonprofit organization where they volunteer. In 2010, Humana associate Brian Eshleman of Ohio won the grant, which he donated to Cleveland Clinic Foundation's Caring Canines program. Eshleman's ten-year-old Scottish Terrier, Bailey, is a certified therapy dog, which Eshleman and wife, Kate, bring to the adult palliative medicine floor—providing invaluable emotional support, increasing

FOUR-LEGGED FRIENDS
OF THE FOUNDATION ///

Between 1974 and 2010,
Humana and The Humana
Foundation contributed
$220 million to charitable
initiatives and community
organizations. The Anti-
Cruelty Society, an unlimited-
stay humane society
in Chicago, received a
$100,000 grant to improve
technologies that track pet
abuse trends and target
outreach efforts. Far left:
ACS staff member Amin
Rajput works with a dog
being cared for at the society.
Near left: Staff member
Margaret Barnard uses the
new computer equipment to
update records.

smiles and laughter, and generally reducing anxiety
for patients and their families. "It's amazing to see the
reactions of patients meeting Bailey for the first time and
the smiles he brings to their faces," Eshleman said. "Many
have pets at home and can't bring them into the hospital.
It is very fulfilling for my wife and me to share Bailey with
people that really need joy in their lives."

The Humana Foundation also sponsors the Spirit
of Philanthropy award, which recognizes associates'
exceptional commitment and offers them the opportunity
to select a nonprofit group to receive a $25,000 grant
from the foundation. In October 2010, the Kansas
City Humana Bike MS Team won the award. In 2006,
the team started with just two riders, Jerry James and
Frank Quinlan. Since then, 164 Humana riders have
participated with Team Humana and have raised more

than $100,000 for the National Multiple Sclerosis Society
Mid-America Chapter through non-work fundraisers.
"Our people believe it is important to invest time and
money in the community in which we live and thrive. We
are surprised and honored to receive this award and
will give the donation to the MS 150 chapter of Greater
Kansas City," said Jeremy Gaskill, market president,
Kansas and Missouri. "This award is a great reflection of
the commitment our associates have to the Kansas City
market, and I am so proud of their work."

Humana also sponsors the "Starlight Award"
in communities where it operates, in which it awards
$10,000 to volunteers age sixty-five and older to
donate to the charity of their choice. In 2009, F. Warren
Pitcher, a senior volunteer with the Blood Center of
Iowa, received the award in the Des Moines area.

**ALWAYS STAYING
PATIENT-FOCUSED ///**

The daily involvement of
clinicians in considering
members' individual
needs supports
Humana's results-driven
goal of improving its
customers' health and
well-being. Teresa Ramos,
MD, a regional medical
director based out of
Humana's Chicago office,
meets with members of
the Medicare team to
discuss program updates.

Pitcher is a lifelong blood donor, blood drive organizer, and transportation volunteer for the Blood Center of Iowa, which received a $10,000 grant in his name. Throughout his lifetime, Pitcher has donated more than nine gallons of blood, which has helped more than two hundred hospital patients. Additionally, his leadership as an organizer for his church-sponsored blood drives over the last nine years has assisted the Blood Center in collecting more than one hundred thousand units of blood annually. Pitcher also volunteers his time to help transport blood to hospitals across the state of Iowa. "I am thrilled to receive this award," Pitcher said. "I feel honored to be recognized for my efforts, but truly my joy comes from knowing that I'm helping someone in our community. I truly believe that blood donation saves lives, and I am happy to be able to be a part of this great program in our community."

Separately, Humana sponsors a one-time, $100,000 transformational grant to a nonprofit in areas where it has major operations. In 2011, the Humana Communities Benefit program was offered in eight U.S. cities. "Giving through the company as well as the foundation allows our local market leaders to be more engaged and invite community leaders to join them in some of the conversation about our grant-making," Judd explained. Local Humana business leaders issue a request for proposal, narrow the competition down to three nonprofits, and then assemble a panel of community business leaders to judge presentations by the three finalists. A winner is chosen, and the two finalists receive smaller grants.

In 2009, Atlanta leaders awarded the grant to the Atlanta Community Food Bank, which serves more than four hundred thousand residents, half of whom are children. The food bank distributes nearly two million pounds of food and grocery items to more than

seven hundred nonprofit partner agencies in thirty-eight counties every month. The grant allowed the organization to create a healthy food co-op, offering residents rarely donated food such as shelf-stable milk, peanut butter, canned and frozen meats, and other high-protein foods. "The Atlanta Community Food Bank is so thankful to Humana for the grant that will allow us to help secure more food for individuals, families, and communities in Atlanta and northern Georgia," said Bill Bolling, executive director of the Atlanta Community Food Bank. "These funds will go a long way in making a difference, most notably helping to create a new food co-op that will help hundreds of thousands of vulnerable Georgians make healthy food choices that are usually out of their reach."

ENVIRONMENTAL INITIATIVES

Humana sponsors a range of other initiatives through its Corporate Social Responsibility platform of Healthy People, Healthy Planet, and Healthy Performance. For example, the company participates in the Carbon Disclosure Project (CDP), an independent nonprofit organization that holds the world's largest database of corporate climate change information. The data is obtained from responses to CDP's annual information requests, issued on behalf of institutional investors, purchasing organizations, and government bodies. Since its formation in 2000, CDP has become the gold standard for carbon disclosure methodology and process, providing primary climate change data to the global marketplace. In 2009, Humana received a high ranking on the CDP Leadership Index.

Meanwhile, Humana's Kansas City market office is making a sustainable workplace a reality. The Kansas City Green Team, formed in April 2008, launched a broad recycling program that includes plastic bottles and shopping bags, cardboard, tin and aluminum cans,

the environment. From 2007 to 2010, Humana has been recognized as a leader in environmental protection by being listed among select companies on the Dow Jones Sustainability Index. Similarly, the company was named the leader in the health benefits industry by *Corporate Responsibility Officer* magazine for a variety of programs designed to preserve the well-being of the planet. In addition, KLD Research & Analytics, Inc. included Humana in six of its stock indexes targeting socially conscious investors in 2008. In 2011, the company headquarters won Energy Star certification from the EPA, scoring in the top 25 percent based on the National Energy Performance rating system.

HUMANA HABITAT ///

Habitat for Humanity has been a longtime beneficiary of Humana associates' time and The Humana Foundation's resources. In 2009, Heartland Habitat for Humanity received $100,000 from Humana's Kansas City benefits grant competition. More than six hundred Humana associates have worked on Habitat projects throughout Louisville since 2003.

HEALTH, WELLNESS, AND KIDS

In April 2005, Mike McCallister became chairman of the Humana Foundation Board. Charitable efforts in recent years have focused greater attention on improving health and well-being, aligning more closely with the company's larger mission. Although the foundation had long supported efforts to prevent teen smoking, it wanted to place a greater emphasis on health and wellness for children.

The Humana Foundation's Healthy Environment & Active Lifestyles Through Education (HEALThE) Schools program is a comprehensive effort in several Jefferson County Public Schools to improve student health. In the program's first year, sugary drinks were removed from vending machines, and Humana supplied games to boost physical activity. At Rangeland Elementary, for example, where nine in ten students are eligible for a free or reduced-cost lunch, Humana donated $60,000 to equip the school's new Innovation Lab and provide healthy after-school snacks. Each day, more than one hundred students use the lab, which offers a dozen video game stations that

ink-jet cartridges, compact fluorescent bulbs (CFLs), and alkaline batteries. Team members have hosted a clothing drive for Big Brothers Big Sisters as well as an e-recycling drive, and they recently convinced Humana's landlord to install a recycling receptacle in the parking lot, allowing 180 fellow tenants to join the green revolution. Future plans include a carpooling program, recycling for cell phones and eyeglasses, and an internal bulletin board that will let associates exchange unwanted or unneeded items with each other rather than send them to the landfill. The program is expected to become a model for other Humana offices.

Across the company, Humana has challenged associates to replace at least one incandescent bulb at home with a CFL and make other changes at home to save energy. Since 2007, associates have saved a potential $2,998,241 in energy costs while keeping nearly 38,478,282 pounds of greenhouse gases out of

HEALTHY KIDS AND ADULTS ///

Wellness literacy for both children and adults is a primary focus for The Humana Foundation. Its Wellness Information Zone initiative, right bottom, was launched in 2007 to provide free, reliable health information in multiple languages the pedometer program Horsepower Challenge, right top, keeps kids moving by offering fun, school-based incentives to track and increase the number of steps they take each day. Opposite: Humana board member David A. Jones, Jr., receives some coaching on games used as part of the HEALThE Schools program from children who attend Rangeland Elementary in Louisville. As a personification of Humana's emerging well-being orientation, in 2009 Jones Jr.—then Humana's board chair—won a bronze medal in the triathlon at the National Senior Games for the fifty to fifty-four age group. The games have been sponsored by Humana since 2007.

include programs such as Dance Dance Revolution, Wii Sports, and Wii Fit. There are also six stationary exercise bikes with accompanying virtual-reality screens that allow students to ride and track their progress. Students play for forty-five minutes at a time. "The kids are really perspiring by the time they get out of there," Shemaine Bridges, Rangeland's health and fitness coordinator, told the Louisville *Courier-Journal* in 2009. "They're getting their energy and stress out so they are able to focus a little more in the classroom once they leave." Students and teachers also wear pedometers to track the distances they walk each day.

"We've placed the development of fitness game labs in those schools, where students can participate at least once a week," said Judd. "We are also funding some of the in-school programming that promotes exercise and eating right. There's after-school programming that all kids can engage in, so it might be yoga classes or healthy cooking classes. The goal is to make students more active and raise their awareness about health. We want 'healthy to be fun and fun to be healthy.' We will look to see if the effort drives behavior change, and if it does, we are going to test it in other schools." After the program's first year in two schools, the students' awareness of healthy behaviors grew, and science grades rose 20 percent.

In 2011, the HEALThE Schools program launched a web site to encourage students to be more aware of the daily choices that influence their health. A "diary" page allows students to input information about what they are eating and their physical activity, and the data is aggregated and presented on a "report card" page so schools can monitor their progress in achieving a healthy student body. Schools can also use information to select or modify school health programs and to apply for school health grants. "Each child has an online avatar, and if they make healthier choices their avatar will grow," said Judd. "Their avatar also relates to the teachers' and parents' avatars, so there's a little competition going on, and all of them relate to a bar above their heads representing a perfect score. We are testing it as a pilot to capture data to see if the program encourages healthy behaviors."

The Humana Foundation is also focused on health literacy for adults. In 2007, it created the Wellness Information Zone to connect individuals and their families to free, reliable health information in everyday language. The initiative is designed for easy health reference through the use of a web site—wellzone.org—as well

as health information kiosks and trained guides. A pilot initiative was launched in Atlanta, and partners include the National Center for Family Literacy and the YMCA. The project has since expanded to sites in Houston and Louisville, including libraries, community centers, health clinics, elementary schools, and YMCAs. "The web site is targeted toward the 90 million Americans who have low health literacy and trouble identifying and understanding health information," Judd said. "This is a site that makes it easier for you to get that information." In 2010, The Humana Foundation formed a partnership with the University of Kentucky to create the first statewide health literacy conference in Kentucky, which led to the statewide Health Literacy Kentucky coalition.

Humana's efforts in corporate citizenship and philanthropy are an extension of the company's underlying values. "Our giving demonstrates our values to all of our stakeholders—our associates, clients, shareholders, and the communities in which we operate," said McCallister. "It helps us attract, motivate, and inspire

excellent associates; it shows clients we are serious about influencing positive change; and it aligns our firm with leaders in the larger corporate community who have recognized the powerful impact they can make through social responsibility and philanthropic programs. I think it is important for Humana to give back to the communities in which our company operates. The company and The Humana Foundation believe our values and our business are well served when we help improve the quality of life where we can."

Most important, the company's innovations and contributions, especially in health literacy and wellness, reflect the future of Humana's business. "Our dream as a company is to foster lifelong well-being through a new world of health benefits," McCallister said. "We will continue to innovate and develop the tools, guidance, and positive incentives that empower and encourage people to take control of their health and ultimately their well-being." The company's legacy— fifty years of helping people—has remained constant through the evolutions of its strategy, business models, and customer base. At the same time, its philanthropic efforts have broadened over time to embrace people and programs as far afield as Eastern Europe. Built on a bedrock of integrity, embodying the golden rule in its relationships with partners and customers, and allowing its associates to "earn and learn" as they build their careers, Humana confronts the next half-century as dedicated as ever to fostering transformative change. "We are on a journey," McCallister said, "that we believe will profoundly alter the landscape of health care delivery in the U.S."